HAL LEONARD

JAZZ PIANO METHOD

Stylings

BY MARK DAVIS

PLAYBACK+
Speed • Pitch • Balance • Loop

To access audio visit:
www.halleonard.com/mylibrary

Enter Code
4350-7361-5534-9831

ISBN 978-1-4803-9800-9

HAL•LEONARD®

Visit Hal Leonard Online at
www.halleonard.com

Contact us:
Hal Leonard
7777 West Bluemound Road
Milwaukee, WI 53213
Email: info@halleonard.com

In Europe, contact:
Hal Leonard Europe Limited
42 Wigmore Street
Marylebone, London, W1U 2RN
Email: info@halleonardeurope.com

In Australia, contact:
Hal Leonard Australia Pty. Ltd.
4 Lentara Court
Cheltenham, Victoria, 3192 Australia
Email: info@halleonard.com.au

CONTENTS

INTRODUCTION

Learning to play jazz can be exciting and fun, but it can also be bewildering and frustrating at times. This method will guide you step by step through the complexities of the music and show you ways to practice that will enable you to play piano in an authentic jazz style. Ultimately, this will allow you to express yourself and find your individual voice. It is important to keep in mind that this is a long road, but one that will yield many rewards along the way.

Only basic piano proficiency and rudimentary music reading are required to begin this study. Following the practice suggestions in this book will help you develop essential jazz techniques that will put you on the road to becoming a skilled jazz pianist. Listening is as important as practicing. Take in live performances and analyze recordings. Go to jam sessions, find others who want to get together and play, and get to know experienced musicians who can answer your questions. I also recommend that you find a good private teacher who can help guide you. Be patient, enjoy the process of learning, and understand that there is no end; there is always more to know, always new things to discover. This is what makes playing jazz piano such a fascinating endeavor.

Chapter 1
GETTING STARTED

PRACTICE TIPS

Move through this book in sequence. Take time to master each exercise before moving on. Keep a practice log of your activities and the time you spend on each exercise, technique, or concept. Daily practice is the key to success. Take the time to learn fingerings that will allow you to play fluently. It is also important to practice with a steady pulse. Practice with a metronome and play along with the recorded examples to develop the strong sense of time you will need to play effectively, whether in a group or as a soloist. Always choose a tempo that allows you to play with accuracy. If you are making lots of mistakes because of the tempo, slow it down and then gradually work your way up. Learn to play *everything* you practice from memory. Resist the urge to play exercises or tunes over and over by reading them. You need to free yourself from the written music in order to become an improviser. As you move through the book, you will undoubtedly need to go back and review certain sections and exercises. This is all part of the process.

DEVELOPING YOUR EAR

Think of a simple melody; it could be "Mary Had a Little Lamb" or "Happy Birthday to You." Randomly pick a starting note on the piano and try your best to play the song. Once you have played it successfully, start on a different note and try to play the song. This is a great way to develop your ear. It also acquaints you with **transposition***, the process of moving a group of notes to another key. It's also never too soon to try to play things you hear on recordings, whether it's a phrase, an entire melody, or a solo. The act of notating what you hear is called **transcribing**. Mimicking other players is one of the main ways jazz musicians learn, but it takes practice to get good at it. You may want to try to play some of the recorded examples in this book by ear and then check your accuracy with the notation in the book. Eventually, you will be able to transcribe things you hear on your favorite jazz recordings and this will help your musicianship immensely.

RECOMMENDED LISTENING

In order to play jazz, you need to be listening to it – a lot! You must immerse yourself in the music. Listening to all styles of music and to different instrumentalists and vocalists will be a great source of inspiration. The recordings of Louis Armstrong, Charlie Parker, and John Coltrane are essential, and listening to them will give you an excellent historical overview. The following list, however, focuses on some of the historically important jazz pianists and those who are most relevant to the topics in this book. Check out as many of them as you can. For an overview of the history of jazz piano, I suggest you listen to solo recordings by Art Tatum, Bud Powell from 1953 or before (considered by many to be his best period), and McCoy Tyner from the 1960s. Familiarizing yourself with the pianists below will give you a basis for appreciating and assessing the styles of the many incredible pianists who have come to prominence in more recent years.

Jelly Roll Morton (1890-1941)	George Shearing (1919-2011)	Buddy Montgomery (1930-2009)
James P. Johnson (1894-1955)	John Lewis (1920-2001)	Tommy Flanagan (1930-2001)
Duke Ellington (1899-1974)	Erroll Garner (1921-1977)	Ahmad Jamal (b. 1930)
Earl Hines (1903-1983)	Al Haig (1922-1982)	Sonny Clark (1931-1963)
Fats Waller (1904-1943)	Red Garland (1923-1984)	Wynton Kelly (1931-1971)
Count Basie (1904-1984)	Bud Powell (1924-1966)	Phineas Newborn, Jr. (1931-1989)
Art Tatum (1909-1956)	Oscar Peterson (1925-2007)	Joe Zawinul (1932-2007)
Teddy Wilson (1912-1986)	Kenny Drew (1928-1993)	Cedar Walton (1934-2013)
Tadd Dameron (1917-1965)	Horace Silver (1928-2014)	Bobby Timmons (1935-1974)
Thelonious Monk (1917-1982)	Hampton Hawes (1928-1977)	McCoy Tyner (b. 1938)
Hank Jones (1918-2010)	Bill Evans (1929-1980)	Herbie Hancock (b. 1940)
Nat "King" Cole (1919-1965)	Barry Harris (b. 1929)	Chick Corea (b. 1941)

*The terms in bold are defined in the glossary.

STYLES

As you listen, take note of the various styles you hear. You will begin to recognize certain characteristics that are indicative of the time period in which a recording was made. Early jazz pianists, for example, often played **stride** with the left hand, a technique that usually involved playing a low note on the first and third beats and a middle register **chord** on the second and fourth beats of each measure. Pianists of each era used distinctive, identifiable techniques.

You will also hear a variety of rhythmic styles. The basic **feel** in jazz has been **swing**, but jazz also makes use of a wide array of grooves that include Latin, rock, and funk. The **bossa nova** of Brazil has been one of the most prevalent Latin styles that jazz musicians have incorporated. Notice how the music sounds at different tempos, from slow ballads to up-tempo burners. Historically, most jazz has been played in 4/4 time signature, however 3/4, 6/8, and other so-called "odd meters" such as 5/4 and 7/4 are also used.

JAZZ STANDARDS

A jazz **standard** is a tune that you are expected to know, to have in your repertoire, as a jazz musician. Many of them were composed for musicals or movies and some were written by jazz musicians. Experienced jazz musicians have hundreds of tunes memorized. You should make a point of listening to recordings of standards. Listen to classic versions to learn the basic tune, then listen to many different versions of the same song to understand how different players give it their own unique treatment. If it is a song with lyrics, find a vocal version by someone like Frank Sinatra or Ella Fitzgerald. Knowing the words can help you remember the melody and interpret the song.

Here is a list of some of the most important tunes to know. You may choose to start with the tunes I have marked with a letter B. These tunes are a bit easier for a beginner to learn. Tunes followed by an asterisk are among the most frequently played and, therefore, essential. This list is subjective since the musicians you play with and the musical circles you get into will dictate which tunes are important for you to know. You will likely find there are tunes that are not on this list that will become part of your repertoire.

Afternoon in Paris (B)

Ain't Misbehavin'

Airegin

Alice in Wonderland

All Blues (B) *

All of Me

All of You

All the Things You Are *

Almost Like Being in Love (B)

Alone Together *

Along Came Betty

Angel Eyes

April in Paris

Autumn Leaves (B) *

Beatrice

Beautiful Friendship

Beautiful Love

Black Orpheus (also called
A Day in the Life of a Fool
or Manhã de Carnaval) (B)

Blue Bossa (B) *

Blue Skies

Body and Soul *

Bolivia

But Beautiful

But Not for Me

Bye Bye Blackbird (B) *

Cantaloupe Island (B) *

Caravan *

Ceora

Cherokee *

Come Rain or Come Shine

Con Alma

Confirmation

Corcovado (also called
Quiet Nights of Quiet Stars) *

Darn That Dream

Days of Wine and Roses *

Dolphin Dance

Don't Blame Me

Don't Get Around Much Anymore

Donna Lee (based on the chord
progression of Indiana (Back Home
Again in Indiana))

Doxy (B) *

East of the Sun (and West of the Moon)

Easy Living

Easy to Love

Embraceable You

Emily

Everything Happens to Me

Falling in Love with Love (B)

Fly Me to the Moon (B)

A Foggy Day

Footprints (B) *

Four *

Gentle Rain

Georgia on My Mind

Giant Steps *

The Girl from Ipanema *

God Bless' the Child

Gone with the Wind

Good Bait

Green Dolphin Street (also called On
Green Dolphin Street) (B) *

Groovin' High

Half Nelson (based on the chord progression of Lady Bird)

Have You Met Miss Jones? (B) *

Here's That Rainy Day

Hi-Fly

Honeysuckle Rose (B)

How Deep Is the Ocean?

How High the Moon (B) *

How Insensitive

I Can't Get Started (B) *

I Didn't Know What Time It Was

I Fall in Love Too Easily

I Got Rhythm (B) *

I Hear a Rhapsody

I Love You *

I Mean You

I Remember You *

I Should Care

I Thought About You

I'll Remember April (B) *

I'm Getting Sentimental Over You

I'm Old Fashioned

I've Grown Accustomed to Her Face

I've Never Been in Love Before

If I Should Lose You *

If I Were a Bell

If You Could See Me Now

Impressions (based on the chord progression of So What) (B) *

In a Mellow Tone

In a Sentimental Mood *

In Walked Bud

In Your Own Sweet Way

Indiana (Back Home Again in Indiana)

Inner Urge

Invitation *

It Could Happen to You *

It Don't Mean a Thing

It's You or No One

Joy Spring

Just Friends *

Just in Time

Just One of Those Things

Just You, Just Me

Killer Joe

Lady Bird (B) *

Laura

Lazy Bird

Like Someone in Love *

Little Sunflower (B)

Love for Sale

Lover

Lover Come Back to Me

Lover Man (B)

Lullaby of Birdland

Lush Life

Maiden Voyage (B)

Meditation

Milestones (There are two different tunes with this title, referred to as the old version and new version. Both are good to know.)

Misty (B) *

Moanin'

Moment's Notice

Moonlight in Vermont

The More I See You

My Foolish Heart

My Funny Valentine *

My Little Suede Shoes (B)

My One and Only Love

My Romance *

My Shining Hour *

Naima

Nancy with the Laughing Face

Nardis

The Nearness of You

Nica's Dream

Night and Day*

The Night Has a Thousand Eyes

A Night in Tunisia (B) *

Old Devil Moon

Old Folks

One Note Samba

Ornithology (based on the chord progression of How High the Moon) *

Our Love Is Here to Stay

Out of Nowhere (B) *

Over the Rainbow (also called Somewhere Over the Rainbow)

Pent-Up House (B)

Perdido (B)

Polka Dots and Moonbeams

Prelude to a Kiss

Recorda Me (B) *

'Round Midnight*

Satin Doll (B) *

Scrapple from the Apple (B) *

Secret Love

Seven Steps to Heaven

The Shadow of Your Smile

Skylark

Smile

So What (B) *

Softly, as in a Morning Sunrise (B) *

Solar (B) *

Someday My Prince Will Come (B) *

Song for My Father (B) *

The Song Is You

Sophisticated Lady

Soul Eyes

Speak Low *

St. Thomas (B) *

Stablemates

Star Eyes *

Stardust

Stella by Starlight *

Sugar (B)

Summertime (B) *

Sweet and Lovely

Sweet Georgia Brown

Take the "A" Train (B) *

Tenderly

There Is No Greater Love *

There Will Never Be Another You *

These Foolish Things

Triste

Tune-Up (B)

Up Jumped Spring

Watermelon Man (B)

Wave

The Way You Look Tonight *

Well You Needn't (B) *
What Is This Thing Called Love? (B) *
What's New?
When Lights Are Low
Whisper Not *
Willow Weep for Me
Without a Song
Woody'n You
Work Song (B)
Yardbird Suite *
Yesterdays *
You and the Night and the Music
You Don't Know What Love Is

You Go to My Head
You Stepped Out of a Dream *
You'd Be So Nice to Come Home To
You've Changed

Tunes based on the blues

Au Privave *
Billie's Bounce *
Blue Monk (B) *
Now's the Time (B) *
Sonnymoon for Two (B)
Tenor Madness (B) *

Tunes based on the minor blues

Mr. P.C. (B) *
Birk's Works (B)

Tunes based on the chords of "I Got Rhythm"

Anthropology *
Moose the Mooche
Oleo (B) *
Rhythm-a-Ning
The Theme (B) *

THE FORM OF A TUNE

Form refers to the length and structure of a jazz tune when played once through, not including an **intro** or special ending. A **blues (blues progression)** is typically 12 measures (12 bars) long. Most standards are 32 measures in length, but other structures are used as well. A 32-bar tune can be divided into four eight-measure sections. When referring to these sections, we assign letters of the alphabet beginning with the letter A. The same letter is used for repeated or nearly identical sections, and subsequent letters of the alphabet are used for sections that are different. "(Somewhere) Over the Rainbow" is a good example of the most common form, AABA. The B section of an AABA form is called the **bridge**. Other common forms are ABAC (e.g., "Green Dolphin Street") and ABCD (e.g., "My Shining Hour").

THE STRUCTURE OF A TYPICAL JAZZ PERFORMANCE

Although a performance by a **big band** (an ensemble of 10 or more members) can be a bit more complex, a small jazz group usually adheres to a rather formulaic format. A tune often begins with an eight-measure introduction (intro). A **ballad** (a slow tune) is usually introduced with a four-bar intro. After the intro, the melody of the tune, known as the **head**, is played once before solos begin (twice on short forms). Each member of the group is generally given the opportunity to improvise a solo with rhythm section accompaniment. One time through the form of a tune is called a **chorus**, and each musician usually improvises a few choruses before passing off to the next soloist. Horns usually solo first, followed by the pianist, the bassist, and the drummer. The drummer sometimes takes a solo of one or more unaccompanied choruses or may alternate brief solos with one or more members of the group, usually in segments of four or eight measures, a technique called **trading fours** or **trading eights**. The form of the tune is retained during this process. After everyone has soloed, the head is played again, often followed by a special ending.

THE PIANIST'S ROLE IN A JAZZ GROUP

We are responsible for playing chords that accompany the melody of the song and the improvised solos of the members of the group. This is commonly referred to as **comping**. We are often part of a **rhythm section** that includes bass and drums, but might also include percussion and/or guitar. Pianists improvise solos that are often linear, horn-like melodic lines played by the right hand while they "comp" with their left hand. We are often in charge of setting up tunes with an intro and we sometimes need to lead the group in an ending.

Chapter 2
ESSENTIAL THEORY

THE CHROMATIC SCALE

Most melodies are based on scales, and chords come from scales as well. **Scales** are groups of notes arranged in ascending or descending order. When we use scales to improvise melodies, we can move up or down or skip around. Chords can be created by combining three or more notes from a scale. Knowing scales is essential.

We begin with what one might consider the most important scale. It is a scale that contains everything, our musical universe. It is called the **chromatic scale**. It is constructed entirely in **half steps** and it contains all 12 notes. There is only one chromatic scale; everything you play is part of the chromatic scale. Here it is with right-hand fingering.

TRACK 1

Practice: Use a metronome and set the tempo to 72 beats per minute or slower. Improvise melodies with your right hand by moving up and down the chromatic scale. Play quarter notes and focus on being rhythmically accurate; try to make each note you play coincide exactly with the click of the metronome. Next, try improvising using only eighth notes. Once you are comfortable with this, try switching between quarter notes and eighth notes every two measures. This will help you develop a stronger sense of time. Work your way up to faster metronome settings. Here is an example of chromatic scale improvisation.

TRACK 2

THE WHOLE TONE SCALE

Next, play every other note of the chromatic scale. You are now playing a six-note scale known as the **whole tone scale**. It is built entirely in **whole steps**. Here is the whole tone scale starting on C.

TRACK 3

Next, play all the notes you skipped. This forms a different whole tone scale. There are only two whole tone scales. You can start a whole tone scale on any note, but you will find that what you play is always part of one or the other. Here is the whole tone scale starting on B.

TRACK 4

Practice: Try improvising with each of the two whole tone scales using a metronome and the same rhythmic approach you used with the chromatic scale. Here is an example of improvisation based on the C whole tone scale.

TRACK 5

THE MAJOR SCALE

At this point, you have become familiar with half steps and whole steps. These are the intervals that are used to form the **major scale**. You can start on any note and ascend using the following sequence of whole steps and half steps to form a major scale: whole step–whole step–half step–whole step–whole step–whole step–half step. The following example shows the C major scale.

TRACK 6

You can see that a seven-note scale was formed. The final half step brings you back to the same note you started on, but an octave higher.

You need to be able to play the major scale in all 12 keys. If you remember the pattern of whole steps and half steps, you will be able to correctly form the scale starting on any note in the chromatic scale.

Practice: Play the major scales with eighth notes as shown below. Pick a starting note, play up the scale to the seventh **degree** (seventh note of the scale), and come back down. Since most of your melodic playing will be done by the right hand, only those fingerings are shown. Use the thumb to begin scales that start on a white note and use the second finger to begin scales that start on a black note. Start slowly, use a metronome, and gradually increase the tempo as you are able. Here is the major scale transposed to all 12 keys.

TRACK 7

INTERVALS

It is important to understand how we describe distances between notes. The major scale is the basis for how these **intervals** are named. The first degree (note) of a major scale is known as the **tonic**. The following are terms used to describe the various intervals. The terms in parentheses are part of the proper name, but are often omitted in common usage.

- Tonic up to the flatted or lowered second degree of a major scale is a minor 2nd.

- Tonic up to the second degree of a major scale is a (major) 2nd.

- Tonic up to the flatted or lowered third degree of a major scale is a minor 3rd.

- Tonic up to the third degree of a major scale is a (major) 3rd.

- Tonic up to the fourth degree of a major scale is a (perfect) 4th.

- Tonic up to the sharped or raised fourth degree of a major scale is an augmented 4th. This is the same distance as the tonic up to the flatted or lowered 5th, which is referred to as a diminished 5th. This interval is also called a **tritone** because it is a distance of three whole steps.

- Tonic up to the fifth degree of a major scale is a (perfect) 5th.

- Tonic up to the sharped or raised fifth degree of a major scale is an augmented 5th. This is the same distance as the tonic up to the flatted or lowered 6th, called a minor 6th.

- Tonic up to the sixth degree of a major scale is a (major) 6th.

- Tonic up to the flatted or lowered seventh degree of a major scale is a minor 7th.

- Tonic up to the seventh degree of a major scale is a major 7th.

- Tonic up to the eighth degree of a major scale is a (perfect) octave.

- Tonic up to the flatted or lowered ninth degree of a major scale is a minor 9th.

- Tonic up to the ninth degree of a major scale is a (major) 9th.

We can also describe bigger intervals such as 10ths, 11ths, 12ths, or 13ths.

TRACK 8

Interval Chart

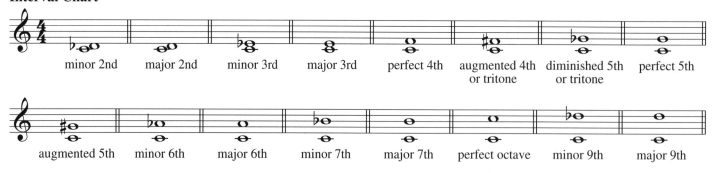

Practice: Play all of these intervals in every key and practice naming them. Understanding intervals will allow you to transpose melodies and chords into any key. You should also try to identify intervals used in familiar tunes. For example, Harold Arlen's "(Somewhere) Over the Rainbow" begins with an octave and Benny Golson's composition "Whisper Not" begins with a perfect 5th. You can also try singing specific intervals and then check your accuracy by playing them on the piano.

THE CYCLE

It is important to memorize a pattern known among jazz musicians as "**the cycle**." It is a series of notes that move up in 4ths until all 12 pitches have been used and the pattern repeats. For this reason, it is also called the Circle of Fourths. Chords often move in the order of the cycle. It also makes a great practice pattern. When jazz musicians learn things in all 12 keys, they usually play them in the order of the cycle.

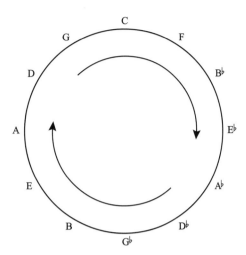

The note you find by moving up a 4th will be the same note you find by moving down a 5th. For example, if I start on C and go up a 4th I get F. If I start on C and go down a 5th, I still get an F. C down to F is a 5th because C is the fifth note of the F major scale. For this reason you can play the cycle going up in 4ths or down in 5ths. The most compact way to play it is to alternate going up and down, as in the example below.

TRACK 9

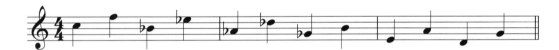

Practice: Start on the lowest C on the piano and play up in 4ths until you reach C again. Then start on the highest C on the piano (the top note) and come down in 5ths. Then play the entire cycle pattern by alternating ascending and descending intervals, as in the example above. As with all the exercises, it is best to practice in time with a metronome.

Up to this point, you have set the metronome to click on each quarter note. Another useful practice technique is to set the metronome to click on every other beat of the tempo you want. Play along with the metronome with the clicks falling on beats two and four when you are playing in a 4/4 time signature. This will prepare you to play with a jazz drummer, who usually plays the hi-hat cymbals on beats 2 and 4. If you tap your foot, it's best to tap on every beat rather than just on 2 and 4. At extremely fast tempos, jazz musicians sometimes tap their foot on just 1 and 3. Here is the major scale showing the metronome clicks on beats 2 and 4.

TRACK 10

SWING EIGHTH NOTES

Throughout the history of jazz, much of the music has been played with a swing feel. This is the typical rhythmic feel of jazz music. An important element of a swing feel is the use of swing eighth notes. Swing eighth notes are typically notated as regular eighth notes to make them easier to read, but when a swing feel is called for, the eighth notes are *played* with a long-short rhythm. Different players have their own individual approaches but, usually, two swing eighth notes are played like a triplet that has its first two notes tied together. This creates a long-short effect.

Here is a line of straight eighth notes. Tunes played with a Latin, funk, rock, or ballad feel usually make use of straight eighth notes.

TRACK 11

If played with a swing feel, the eighth notes in the line above would be played with a long-short rhythm. The following example shows how this sounds. Jazz music is rarely notated using these triplet-based swing rhythms; instead, regular eighth notes are written. If a swing feel is called for, it is up to you to "swing" the eighth notes.

TRACK 12

Careful you don't exaggerate the swing feel too much and sound like this.

TRACK 13

Another important aspect of playing swing eighth notes is the use of accents. The notes that fall squarely on beats 1, 2, 3, and 4 are said to be on the beat, and the notes in between are said to be on the upbeats (also called the "offbeats" or the "ands") of the measure. It is common to put accents on the upbeats.

Practice: Play the C major scale with a swing feel, and accent the upbeats, as in the example below. Exaggerate the accents at first to get the hang of it. Play legato. It is usually best not to use the sustain pedal when you play eighth-note passages. Pedaling can make your lines sound indistinct. After you are comfortable with this exercise, try improvising melodies with the C major scale using swing eighth notes with accents on the upbeats.

TRACK 14

The way swing eighth notes are played varies from player to player. Some tend to play a bit straighter, and some play with a bit more exaggerated "long-short" feel. How accents are used and a pianist's touch on the piano also help define their individual style. In addition, some pianists tend to play just slightly behind the beat to create a more relaxed feel, and some play more on the beat. Playing on top of the beat (a little ahead) creates an edgier feel, but in general, you should avoid this because it can create the feeling that you are rushing. Listen to the greats to help you get a sense of how *you* want to sound.

Practice: It's time to put all of this together. Move through the cycle pattern to play all 12 major scales with correct fingerings. Play root to 7th and back down. Make the last note a quarter note and allow a beat of rest before you move to the next key. Play swing eighth notes with accents on the upbeats. Set the metronome so it is clicking on beats 2 and 4.

Here are the 12 major scales notated with accents.

TRACK 15

Chapter 3
BASIC CHORDS AND VOICINGS

TRIADS

Now that you have become familiar with the major scales, you are ready to learn the basic chords. There are four types of **triads** (chords of three notes that can be stacked in 3rds). In the chart below, the name of the chord type is followed by the formula, followed by chord symbols that are commonly used. The formula numbers correspond to notes of a major scale that are then flatted or sharped as shown. The notes that result are referred to as the root, 3rd, and 5th of the chord. These chord formulas are shown in **root position**, meaning the root is the lowest note. Chord symbols for triads are composed of the root of the chord followed by the symbol that represents the chord type or what we call the **chord quality**. In the examples, C is used as the root, but chords can be played in any of the 12 keys.

major triad	1 3 5	symbols: Cmaj, Cma, CM, C△, C
minor triad	1 ♭3 5	symbols: Cmin, Cmi, Cm, C-
augmented triad	1 3 ♯5	symbol: C+
diminished triad	1 ♭3 ♭5	symbols: C°, Cdim

TRACK 16

Practice: Learn to play major triads in all keys through the cycle. Once you are comfortable with this, learn to play the other chord types (chord qualities) in all keys moving through the cycle. Make sure you are able to play chords with either hand, but when you start to play tunes, much of your chording will be done by the left hand. The standard fingering is 1-3-5 for the right hand, and 5-3-1 for the left hand. You can use the sustain pedal to hold the sound of a chord as you move to the next one; just be sure to clear the pedal each time you play a new chord.

Chords can be played as **inversions**. When a chord is inverted, a note other than the root is in the lowest position. When the 3rd of the chord is the lowest note, the chord is in first inversion. When the 5th of the chord is the lowest note, it is in second inversion. The standard right-hand fingering for a first inversion triad is 1-2-5, and 5-3-1 for the left hand. The standard right-hand fingering for a second inversion triad is 1-3-5, and 5-2-1 for the left hand.

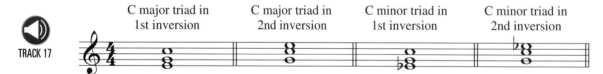

TRACK 17

Practice: Play root-position, first-inversion, and second-inversion major and minor triads in all keys through the cycle as in the example below.

TRACK 18

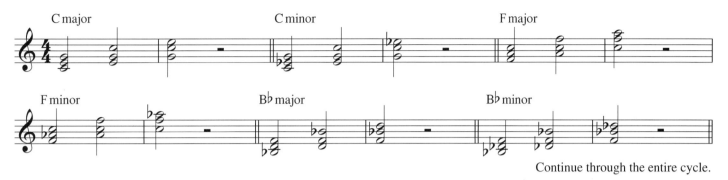

Continue through the entire cycle.

FOUR-NOTE CHORDS

Here are the formulas for **seventh chords**, which all have four notes. Although triads are found in jazz, chords of four or more notes are the norm. This is a distinctive feature of jazz harmony. In the chart below, the name of the chord quality is followed by the formula for the chord in root position, followed by chord symbols that are commonly used. The chord symbols in bold are the ones I use for subsequent examples in this book. The formula numbers correspond to notes of a major scale that are then flatted or sharped as shown. The notes that result are referred to as the root, 3rd, 5th, and 7th of the chord. In the examples, C is used as the root, but chords can be played in any of the 12 keys.

Major 7th	1 3 5 7	symbols: **Cmaj7**, Cma7, CM7, C△7
Dominant 7th	1 3 5 ♭7	symbol: **C7**

Note the difference in the symbols between dominant and major 7th. Beginners sometimes see the symbol for dominant 7th and inadvertently play major 7th instead.

Minor 7th	1 ♭3 5 ♭7	symbols: Cmin7, Cmi7, **Cm7**, C-7
Half-diminished 7th also called Minor 7th(♭5)	1 ♭3 ♭5 ♭7	symbols: **Cø7**, Cø symbols: Cmin7(♭5), Cmi7(♭5), Cm7♭5, C-7(♭5)
Diminished 7th	1 ♭3 ♭5 ♭♭7	symbol: **C°7**

(This chord contains the double-flatted 7th, which is the same note as the 6th.)

Minor-major 7th	1 ♭3 5 7	symbols: Cmin(maj7), C-(△7), **Cm(maj7)**
Major 7th(♯5)	1 3 ♯5 7	symbols: **Cmaj7♯5**, Cma7♯5, CM7♯5, C△7♯5, C△7(+5)

Here are examples of these chords with C as the root.

TRACK 19

Practice: Learn to play major 7th chords in all keys moving through the cycle. Once you can do this, learn dominant 7th and then minor 7th chords. These are the three most common chord qualities in jazz, and learning them will allow you to get started playing lots of tunes. Next, you can move on to learning the other chord types in all keys. The standard fingering for the right hand is 1-2-3-5, and 5-3-2-1 for the left hand. Remember, it is best to practice in tempo. Start slowly. Increase your speed as you become more familiar with the chords.

Seventh chords can be played as inversions. When the 3rd of the chord is the lowest pitch, the chord is in first inversion. When the 5th of the chord is in the bass, it is in second inversion. When the 7th of the chord is in the lowest position, the chord is in third inversion.

Here is an example of C7 in root position and inverted.

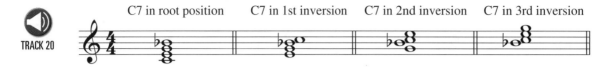

Here are a few more four-note chords you will need to know. The chord symbols in bold are the ones I use for subsequent examples in this book.

Major 6th   1 3 5 6   symbols: **C6**, Cmaj6, C△6
This chord is sometimes used in place of Cmaj7, often when the root is in the melody.

Minor 6th   1 ♭3 5 6   symbols: Cmin6, Cmi6, **Cm6**, C-6
This chord is sometimes used in place of Cm(maj7), often when the root is in the melody.

Dominant 7th(sus4)   1 4 5 ♭7   symbols: C7sus4, **C7sus**, C11
This chord is sometimes used in place of a dominant 7th chord.

Here are examples of these chords with C as the root.

SHELL VOICINGS AND CONCEPTS OF VOICE LEADING

Now that you have become familiar with the basic chords, it's time to start learning some typical jazz voicings. The term **voicing** refers to the particular arrangement of notes in a chord. **Shell voicings** are named as such because they provide just a basic framework, nothing fancy. They make use of just three notes: the root, 3rd, and 7th. The 5th is omitted because it is the least essential note in a 7th chord. There are two types of shell voicings, closed and open. Closed means that the voicing fits within the span of an octave, and open means the interval from the lowest to the highest note of the voicing is more than an octave. Shell voicings are most often played by the left hand to accompany right-hand melodies or to provide the foundation for more complex voicings.

Here is how to play a closed-shell voicing.

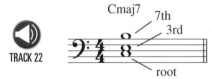

The 3rd and 7th can be flatted as needed to create the various chord qualities, or the 6th can be used in place of the 7th.

To play an open voicing, move the 3rd up an octave to create a voicing that spans a 10th. The following example shows how to play open voicings.

TRACK 24

Unless you have hands like Fats Waller or an NBA basketball player, you are finding that the open chords are either difficult or impossible to reach with your left hand alone. There are several options open to you (pun intended). When you are playing with a bassist, you can leave out the root since a bass line typically provides the root at the start of each chord change. There will also be times when you might choose to play just the 3rd and 7th because the chords are fast moving, and it is just too cumbersome to catch all the roots. Here is an open shell without the root.

TRACK 25

Another possibility is to use the right-hand thumb to play the top note of the open-shell voicings.

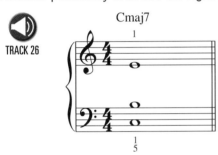
TRACK 26

Although leaving out the root or assisting with the right hand are techniques you will use in the future, as you are getting started, I recommend you play the entire open shell with the left hand alone and break the chord in a rhythmic way.

Play it like this:

TRACK 27

Or play it like this:

TRACK 28

The main reason to use a combination of closed and open chords is to achieve **smooth voice leading**, meaning the notes above the root of each chord are positioned so only minimal movement is required to go from one chord to the next. The next ten examples will get you accustomed to using open- and closed-shell voicings to create smooth voice leading. You can use the broken chord technique for the open chords, but if your reach is big enough to play the notes all at once, go for it! In the recorded examples, I play the broken chords using a swing-eighth-note rhythm.

In the first of these shell voicing exercises, I play dominant 7th chords through the cycle and alternate between open- and closed-shell voicings. The fingering, which you can continue through the whole exercise, makes it easier to go from one chord to the next. Note how the upper two voices move down chromatically as you move through the different keys. You may be used to starting the cycle pattern on C, but these exercises begin on a chord that allows you to play through all 12 keys while remaining in an ideal register.

TRACK 29

The next exercise provides you with a way to practice playing the chords that are closed in the preceding example as open-shell voicings, and those that are open in the preceding example, as closed-shell voicings.

TRACK 30

Now try a similar exercise using major 7th chords. Notice how the upper two voices move in a slightly different way than they did with the dominant exercise.

TRACK 31

Now try it this way.

TRACK 32

Now try the exercise using minor 7th chords. In the example below, I am still following the cycle pattern, but I used **enharmonic equivalents**. Two notes that are identical in pitch, but written differently, are said to be enharmonic. For example, D♭ can be written as a C♯, and G♯ can be written as an A♭. The key signature is one factor that can determine how a note is written. In the next example, I used C♯m7 and F♯m7 in place of D♭m7 and G♭m7, respectively. These are the same chords "spelled" differently. It's important to get used to seeing chords written in different ways.

TRACK 33

Here is another way to play minor 7th chords using open- and closed-shell voicings.

TRACK 34

Lastly, try the exercise alternating between minor 7th and dominant 7th chords. Tracks 35–38 show four different ways to do this using open- and closed-shell voicings.

TRACK 35

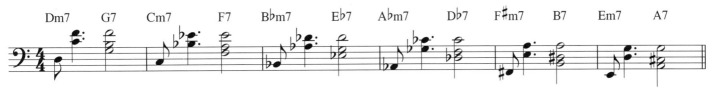

Another way to play minor 7th and dominant 7th chords using open- and closed-shell voicings:

TRACK 36

A third way to play minor 7th and dominant 7th chords using open- and closed-shell voicings:

TRACK 37

A fourth way to play minor 7th and dominant 7th chords using open- and closed-shell voicings:

TRACK 38

Practice: Learn to play the examples on pages 20–22 (Tracks 29–38) from memory. Mastering these chord voicings will prove invaluable when you start learning tunes.

DIATONIC CHORDS

Chords can be built up from each note in a major scale. The seven **diatonic** chords that result serve as the foundation for many songs and common chord progressions. All of the notes of these chords stay within a major scale. In the example below, four-note chords have been formed from the C major scale. Notice that, while all of the notes stay within the C major scale, different chord qualities have resulted. Roman numerals are typically used when describing chord progressions. Often, upper case is used for chords that have a major 3rd, and lower case is used for chords that have a minor 3rd.

TRACK 39

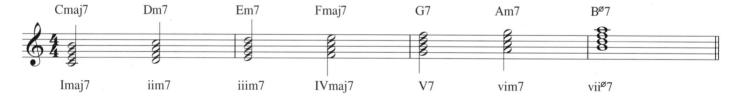

Now try playing the diatonic chords in the key of F major, as in the example below. Notice that all of the notes stay within the F major scale and the same series of chord qualities occurs. The pattern remains the same in every key: major 7th, minor 7th, minor 7th, major 7th, dominant 7th, minor 7th, half-diminished 7th. Memorize this pattern because it will help you to understand chord progressions.

TRACK 40

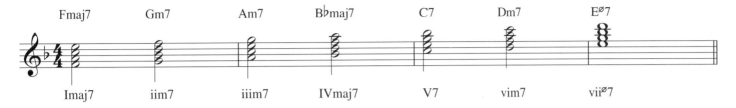

Practice: Play diatonic chords in other keys. Start with common keys like G, B♭, and E♭. Eventually, you should learn to play them in all keys.

THE iim7–V7–Imaj7 PROGRESSION

One of the most frequently used chord sequences in jazz is the iim7–V7–Imaj7 progression. Some jazz tunes are composed mainly of iim7–V7–Imaj7s in different keys. The iim7 and V7 chords set up tension, while the Imaj7 chord is the release and sounds resolved. Here is the progression in the key of C played with shell voicings. Alternating closed and open voicings creates the smoothest voice leading. Notice that the roots of the chords move in the order of the cycle.

Here is the iim7–V7–Imaj7 progression starting with a closed-shell voicing.

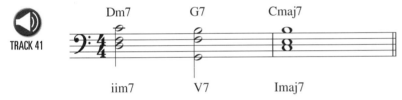

TRACK 41

Here is the same progression starting with an open-shell voicing.

TRACK 42

Practice: Learn to play these chord progressions in all keys. Use broken chords if necessary.

Chapter 4
REPERTOIRE

LEARNING TUNES

It's time to start learning some tunes! Use the list of standards from Chapter 1 to help you decide which ones you would like to begin with. Jazz musicians usually learn tunes either by ear or from a **lead sheet** that shows the melody line and chord symbols. We also refer to a lead sheet or any written arrangement as a **chart**. A book of lead sheets is called a **fake book**, and if you don't already own one, now would be the time to pick one up. *The Real Book* is one of the most popular. Because many fake books notoriously contain mistakes, and since there are many ways to play the same tune, it is important that you listen closely to classic recordings as an aid to learning repertoire.

When jazz musicians say they *know* a tune, they mean they have it memorized. Learning to play repertoire from memory will help you gain the freedom necessary to improvise. Practice just the chords to a tune until you have them thoroughly memorized. I can't stress enough how important it is to really know the form and chords to tunes. You can test yourself in different ways. For example, try reciting the chords to a tune in tempo, or use symbols to write out the chords to a tune you are learning. You will quickly discover which areas need more attention. Also, work carefully on memorizing the melodies to tunes. Learning lyrics can help with this.

Melodies composed by jazz musicians are sometimes played note-for-note the way they were written, but many tunes, especially those with lyrics, are often embellished. The rhythms, too, are frequently altered to sound more jazz-like.

INTERPRETING A LEAD SHEET

On page 25 is a lead sheet for the old standard "My Buddy." Play the melody line with your right hand and add chords underneath with your left. The key signature on a lead sheet affects the melody just as it normally would, but it doesn't affect the chord symbols. For example, if I play a tune with a B♭ in the key signature and come to a Bm7 chord, it does *not* become a B♭m7.

Jazz musicians refer to the chords of a tune as the **changes**. Sometimes you will want to simplify the changes. For example, Gm11 can be played as a Gm7, C13 can be played as C7, and D♭9♯11 can be played as simply D♭7. The 9, 11, and 13 represent **upper extensions**, notes that can be added to a basic four-note chord. Usually, upper extensions are not essential, and it is fine if you don't play them. Often, when they are indicated on a chart, as is the case here, they are notes that are contained in the melody anyway. It is okay to simplify. We will learn more about these extensions in later chapters. The chords in the last measure are played only if you wish to lead back to the **top** (the beginning of the form).

You can use the sustain pedal, but be sure to clear it when chords change. Jazz pianists are more likely to use the pedal on ballads than on swing tunes or up-tempo tunes. Always make sure the melody line and your improvised lines are clear and in the foreground. Playing the left-hand chords softer than the right-hand lines will help you accomplish this.

MY BUDDY

Lyrics by Gus Kahn
Music by Walter Donaldson

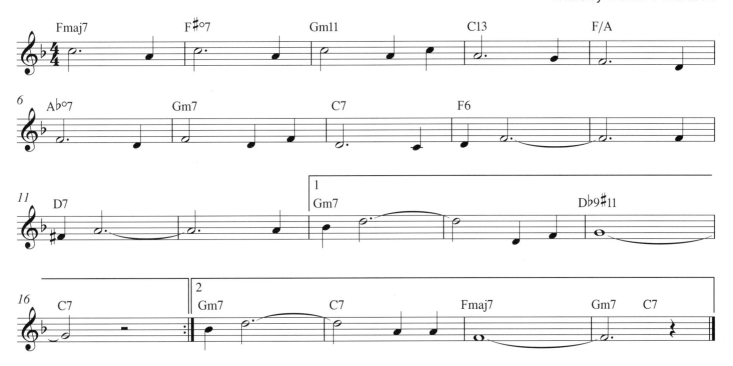

The following example shows how I might play this tune with a swing feel. I used a combination of open- and closed-shell voicings to create smooth voice leading. Sometimes this requires alternating open to closed or closed to open, and sometimes it means playing one or more closed or open chords in a row. I broke up the chords in some spots and added some simple rhythms to keep the tune moving along. I also played parts of the melody using swing-eighth notes and added a bit of **syncopation**, meaning I placed some notes on the offbeats. In measure 5, the symbol F/A indicates you should play an F triad with A as the lowest note (first inversion). Chords that use symbols with a slash are known as **slash chords**. With this type of notation, the chord is indicated to the left of or above the slash, and the note required as the lowest is shown to the right of or below the slash. I put the middle note of this chord up an octave to create an open voicing. I also changed the final Fmaj7 to F6 to better harmonize with the melody. This is often done when the melody note is the root.

MY BUDDY

Lyrics by Gus Kahn
Music by Walter Donaldson

ENDINGS

It is often the responsibility of a jazz pianist to lead the ending of a tune. Some tunes have specific, commonly used endings. As you listen to more recordings and gain experience, you will learn what they are. Many times, however, it will simply be up to you to devise an ending to a tune. It is helpful to develop a "collection" of endings that you can choose from to effectively bring a tune to a close. Here are a couple of ways you might end "My Buddy." These examples can be used to replace the last four bars of the preceding example.

Ending idea 1

TRACK 45

Ending idea 2

TRACK 46

Practice: Transpose these endings to other common keys so that you can use them on other tunes.

APPLYING VOICINGS

As you learn tunes, you will need to choose between the open- and closed-shell voicings. You should begin by looking for the smoothest voice leading possible. For example, if I play Abmaj7 followed by Am7, I would probably play them both either closed or open. When the root movement is a bigger interval, it usually makes sense to alternate closed to open or open to closed to create smooth voice leading. For example, if I play Fm7 followed by Bbm7, I will probably alternate closed to open, or open to closed. In this case, the roots will move a fairly large distance (a 4th or 5th), but the upper voices (the 3rd and 7th), will be positioned to create the least amount of movement possible as you go from one chord to the next.

Sometimes, however, you will find that the smoothest voice leading moves the chords into a register that is too low to sound clear. In the following example, based on the chord progression of Jerome Kern's "All the Things You Are," I started out with a closed chord and then chose voicings to create the smoothest voice movement I could. When I got to measure 9, the smoothest voice leading would have led me to a closed Cm7. I could see that if I continued with this type of voice leading, the chords would soon get too low, so instead I played the Cm7 in measure 9 as an open-shell voicing, allowing the subsequent chords in that section to remain in an ideal register. I also played the F#°7 closed in measure 21 and the Dbm7 open in measure 30 for the same reason.

Practice: Learn to play the following chord progression of "All the Things You Are." You can find the melody in a fake book or learn to play it by ear from a recording. Add the melody with your right hand. Try to bring out the melody by playing it a little louder than the chords. If you need to, break the open-shell voicings or use your right-hand thumb to catch the top note of the chord. Most fake books show an Abmaj7 chord in measure 35. I changed it to Ab6 because the root is in the melody at that point. The chords in the final measure are played only when leading back to the beginning.

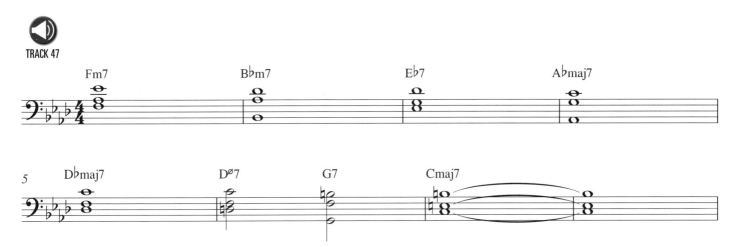

TRACK 47

Practice: Have fun learning more tunes. Experiment with the open- and closed-shell voicings until you find a good balance between smooth voice leading and chords that are in an ideal register.

Chapter 5
BEGINNING IMPROVISATION

THE BLUES SCALE

Most improvised jazz solos are based on scales that relate to the harmony of a tune, but playing with good rhythm is primary. In fact, I would say it is more important than hitting the "right" notes, especially when you first begin to practice improvising. One of the best ways to get started improvising is to use the **blues scale**, shown below in the key of F. The blues scale can be formed by playing the 1st, ♭3rd, 4th, ♭5th, 5th, and ♭7th degrees of a major scale.

TRACK 48

If you leave out the C♭ (♭5), you are left with five notes that form the **minor pentatonic scale**. You can improvise with or without the ♭5th. Because it contains the ♭3rd, the blues scale has a minor sound to it. It works on the blues, but it is also well suited for improvising on minor tunes such as "Summertime," "Sugar," "Moanin'," and "Song for My Father." You can use the blues scale that matches the minor tonality of each of these tunes.

FEELING TIME

When we improvise, we must be able to "feel" how long a measure is. Once you can do this, you can learn to feel durations of two, four, and eight measures. This will enable you to keep your place in a tune without having to count. The following exercises will help you learn to feel time. In the example below, I clap a one-measure rhythm. I then play phrases that use notes from the F blues scale played with that same rhythm, separated by bars of rest. The ♭5th is notated as B♮. **Notice that I play this and all subsequent examples with a swing feel**.

TRACK 49

In this next example, I again play one-measure blues scale phrases based on a rhythm, but this time without the measures of rest.

TRACK 50

Practice: Use the rhythms above to improvise your own F blues scale phrases. Then choose one of the following one-measure rhythms to improvise phrases, first with the bar of separation and then without. After you have tried all these one-bar examples, make up your own. Use a metronome and practice at different tempos.

TRACK 51

(clap)

THE BLUES PROGRESSION

A **progression** or **chord progression** refers to a sequence of chords. The blues progression is the basis for hundreds of tunes, and it is used in a number of musical styles, including blues, jazz, rock, and boogie-woogie. There are countless variations of the blues progression but, in its simplest form, it is 12 measures long and uses three dominant chords that are based upon the first, fourth, and fifth notes of a major scale. Jazz musicians usually refer to this version of the blues as a three-chord blues or a I–IV–V blues. This 12-bar form is typically repeated many times during a performance of a blues. Here is the blues in the key of F, with a suggestion of how to play the chords with shell voicings. If necessary, break the chords or leave out the root. Learn to play this from memory.

TRACK 52

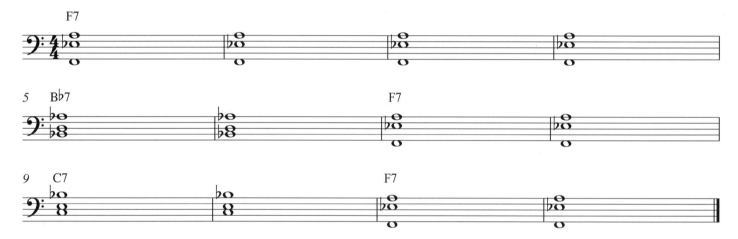

Practice: Improvise right-hand lines with notes from the blues scale while you play the F blues progression with the left hand. Use the F blues scale over the whole blues progression; you don't need to change scales when the chords change. At first, try one-measure phrases like you played earlier, then try longer phrases. Many jazz improvisations are composed mainly of eighth notes, but pianists often emulate the phrasing of horn players, so include some rests as if you were taking breaths.

Here is an example of what your solo might sound like. To keep things a bit simpler, I left out the ♭5.

TRACK 53

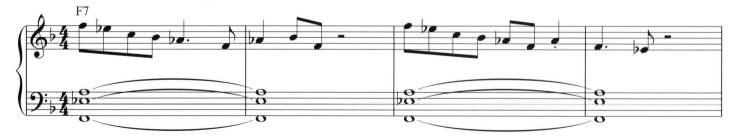

30

Here is another solo on the blues in F. I play two choruses and, this time, I have included the ♭5 (notated as B♮). I have also included more syncopation and less predictable phrasing. On the recorded example, and on subsequent recorded examples, I vary the left-hand comping rhythms a bit. We will discuss this further in Chapter 8.

TRACK 54

Here is the basic blues progression written with Roman numerals. I have included a couple of common variations. You can play IV7 for measure 10, and V7 is often used for measure 12 to lead back to the beginning of the form.

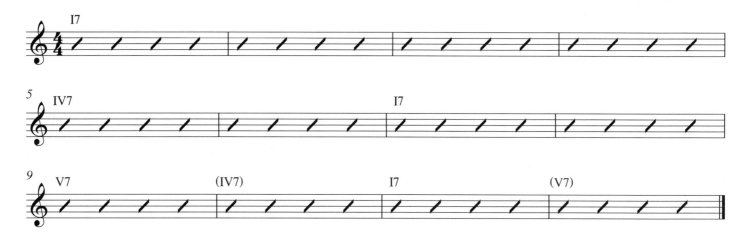

Practice: Use the formula above to transpose the blues progression into other keys. Jazz musicians most frequently choose the keys F, B♭, and C for the blues. Transpose the blues scale as well, and practice improvising in these keys. Improvisation, like any other skill, improves with practice. Play with bass and drum accompaniment as often as you can. When possible, use live musicians. Otherwise, recorded play-alongs or computer apps that simulate rhythm sections are available.

Here are chord charts for the blues in B♭ and C. I have included the IV7 chord in measure 10. The V7 chord in measure 12 is used only when leading back to the beginning of the form. To end the tune, stay on the I7 chord in measure 12.

B♭ Blues Progression (improvise with the B♭ blues scale: B♭–D♭–E♭–E♮–F–A♭–B♭)

TRACK 55

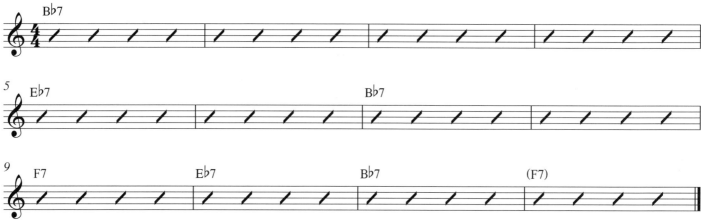

C Blues Progression (improvise with the C blues scale: C–E♭–F–F♯–G–B♭–C)

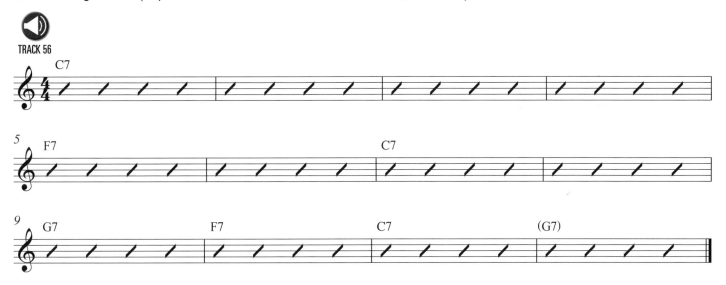

Practice: Create a complete jazz performance by learning a blues head that you can play twice through before you go into your improvisation. After you have improvised, play the head two more times before you end the tune. "Sonnymoon for Two" by Sonny Rollins is a simple blues head that is usually played in B♭ but can easily be transposed to other keys.

IMPROVISING WITH CHORD TONES

Although the blues scale is a great way to get started with improvisation, jazz musicians also employ other techniques that are more closely linked to the harmony of a tune. One method is to use chord tones when you improvise. Below is an example of how that can sound. Notice that I played two choruses and used IV7 for measures 10 and 22, and V7 for measure 12 to lead back to the beginning of the form. To add a little more blues flavor, I sometimes played a grace note from the ♭3rd to the ♮3rd of F7 (e.g., in measures 2 and 4). Occasionally, on the "and" of 4, I played a melody note that is a chord tone of the next chord. One example of this occurs on the "and" of beat 4 in measure 4; I play a D, which is part of the B♭7 chord that immediately follows. This helps give the solo a more syncopated feel.

Practice: Try creating a solo using only the notes that are contained in each chord. Each time a chord changes, you will draw from a new group of notes. Work on the blues progression in F, C, and B♭ to start. Eventually, you can work on other keys and apply this concept to other jazz standards.

Don't be afraid to work things out, to devise preset phrases that you can use in your solos. Sometimes, beginning improvisers are under the impression that because we are improvising, nothing should be worked out in advance. Just the opposite is true. Jazz musicians spend countless hours practicing ideas for solos.

THE MODES OF THE MAJOR SCALE

We have looked at using the blues scale and chord tones in your solos, but jazz musicians also improvise using scales that match the underlying harmony. This usually means we have to change scales every time a chord changes in a tune. Chords come from scales, so when we see a chord symbol on a chart, we need to be able to determine the scale from which the chord is derived. This is how we know which scale to use to improvise. Sometimes, there are several options.

Many of the chords we use come from the diatonic chords that I showed you in Chapter 3. Each of these chords can be viewed as coming from a related mode. **Modes** are scales that are formed by starting on each degree of a "parent" scale. The most commonly used modes come from the major scale and each one has an ancient Greek name. You will see that the first note of a mode is used to describe it, not the tonic of the parent scale. For example, the D Dorian mode starts on D but uses the key signature of the C major scale (parent scale in this case). Here are the modes of the C major scale. Each mode is followed by the chord that is formed by playing its first, third, fifth, and seventh degrees.

TRACK 58

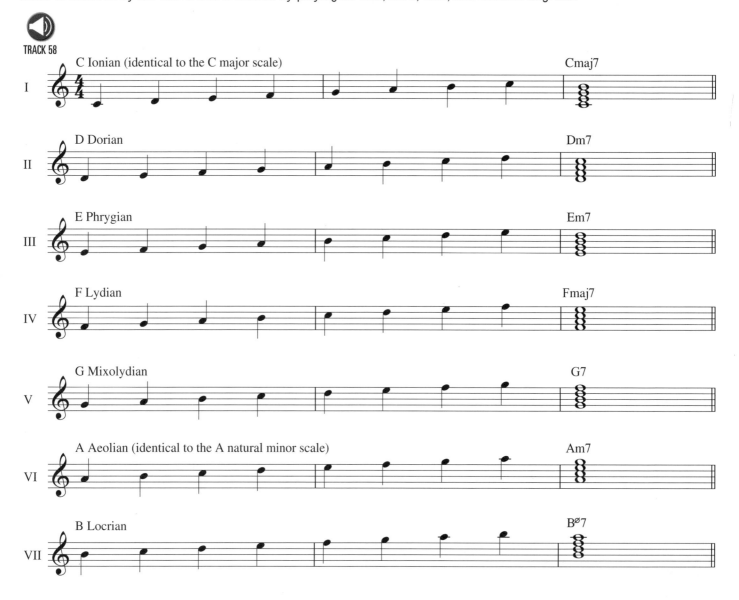

You have already practiced the **Ionian mode** (the major scale). **Mixolydian** and **Dorian** are the most important modes to learn next. You will eventually become familiar with all the modes.

THE MIXOLYDIAN MODE

The fifth mode, the Mixolydian mode, is often the best choice to use when improvising over a dominant chord, and it is sometimes referred to as a dominant scale. It's like a major scale, but with the seventh note flatted.

Practice: Learn to play the Mixolydian mode in all keys. With each mode, play the related dominant chord with the left hand. As with the other examples, play swing eighth notes and accent the upbeats.

Here is the Mixolydian mode in all keys with right-hand fingerings.

TRACK 59

You can use the Mixolydian mode to improvise on the blues. Each time the chords change, switch dominant scales. Try the following exercise based on the blues in F.

TRACK 60

35

When you use Mixolydian modes to improvise on the blues, you don't have to start on the first note of each scale. You can start in the middle and you can jump around to create different intervals. Pay special attention to the fourth note of the Mixolydian mode; it is what we call a **weak tone**, a note in a scale that clashes with a related chord. If you play an F7 chord with your left hand while you play B♭ (the 4th) with your right hand, you will hear the dissonance I am talking about. B♭ is the weak tone in the F Mixolydian mode. You don't need to avoid this note, just make sure you allow it to resolve. When used as a passing tone, you won't even notice the "clash" of this note.

Practice: To get started improvising with Mixolydian modes on the blues, try limiting yourself to just the first, second, and third notes of each mode. Then try using just the third, fourth, and fifth notes. Lastly, try using just the fifth, sixth, and seventh notes. In the following solo on the F blues, I do exactly that. Notice how, in each chorus, I limit myself to just three notes on each chord.

Practice: Once you feel comfortable using three-note segments, improvise on the blues without restriction, using whichever notes you want of the Mixolydian mode. Have fun. Improvising takes lots of practice and experimentation.

Here's an example of what that might sound like.

THE DORIAN MODE

The Dorian mode is another important mode to practice. It is the second mode, and it is often the best choice to use when improvising over a minor 7th chord. It's like a major scale, but with the third and seventh notes flatted. The Dorian mode has no weak tones.

Practice: Learn to play the Dorian mode in all keys, as in the example below. With each mode, play the related minor 7th chord with the left hand.

Here is an improvisation on the chord progression of Miles Davis's "So What," a 32-measure composition with an AABA form that uses just two chords. This tune has long stretches of minor 7th chords that are perfect places to use this mode. The first two A sections are all Dm7, so I used the D Dorian mode (the second mode of C major). The B section (the bridge) is all E♭m7, so there I used the E♭ Dorian mode (the second mode of D♭ major) before switching back to the D Dorian mode for the final A section. To add a little more movement to the harmony, I occasionally used a Dm6 chord in place of Dm7.

TRACK 64

Practice: Improvise with the Dorian mode over long stretches of minor 7th chords. Use a metronome or other accompaniment to help strengthen your sense of time.

THINKING ABOUT SCALES

There are many ways to think about scales when we improvise, and musicians find what works best for them in a given situation. For example, if you are improvising over Cm7–F7, you could use C Dorian on the Cm7, and F Mixolydian on the F7. You could also think more simply and just use the B♭ major scale over both chords, or you could think of using the F Mixolydian over both chords, or C Dorian over both chords. All of these approaches end up giving you the same group of notes; they are just different ways of thinking about them. Get familiar with the modes and you will find that it is easy to go back and forth between different ways of thinking about how scales and chords relate.

Chapter 6
DOMINANT VOCABULARY

THE DOMINANT BEBOP SCALE

Jazz music is very much like language; we even refer to various licks and phrases that we play as **vocabulary**. Think of how a baby learns to speak. First, they babble, just experimenting with sounds, then they begin to learn single words that they repeat over and over again, and soon they begin to connect words and construct sentences that convey more complex ideas. This is exactly how we learn to improvise. Sometimes people refer to a short phrase as a **lick** or an **idea**. In this chapter, I will show you short dominant scale ideas that will function like "words." I'll show you how you can connect these ideas, much like sentences, to create longer lines.

Jazz musicians frequently use descending scales of eighth notes to connect various ideas. When we play scales or any melodic line, we often try to position chord tones on the beat. We sometimes add extra **passing tones** on the upbeats to make this happen. These descending scales with added passing tones are called jazz scales or **bebop scales**.

The example below shows the F7 bebop scale in its basic form. It is a descending F Mixolydian mode with the major 7th added as a passing tone. This added passing tone positions all of the chord tones of F7 on the beats of the measure and the weak tone (the 4th) on an upbeat so that the scale effectively conveys the sound of an F7 chord.

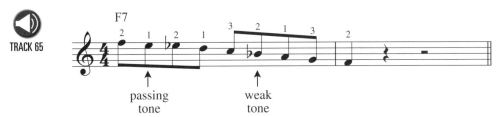

Important point: You can play this scale over Cm7 as well as F7, because these chords form a iim7–V7 progression and they have a related sound and function. Play the following example to hear how this scale works over both chords.

Practice: Learn to play the dominant bebop scale in all keys, as in the following example. Notice that I played each scale over a iim7–V7 in the left hand. When you begin improvising with these, the fingerings will need to be adjusted, but learning these basic fingerings will give you a good starting point. Use the fingerings in parentheses if you want to continue further down the scale.

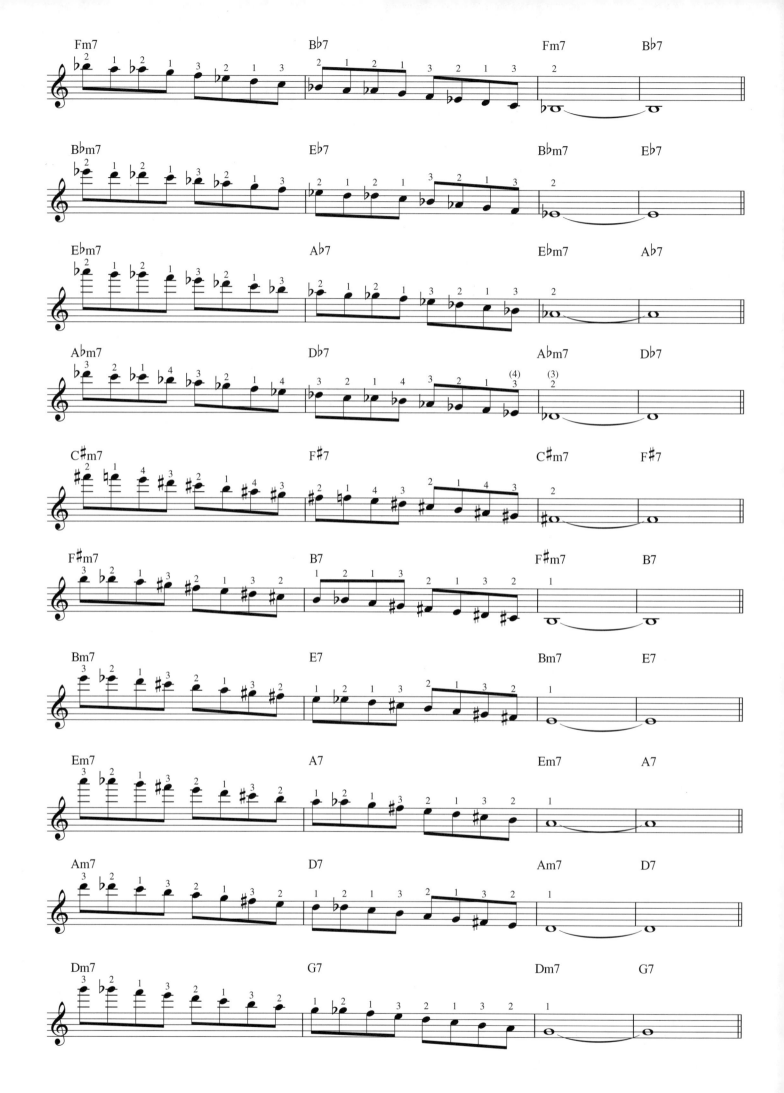

Now learn to play down from any note in the dominant bebop scale (other than from the passing tone (the major 7th)). This involves a lot of tedious practice, but you will be rewarded with the ability to play long, connected lines.

If you descend from the root, 3rd, 5th, or 7th, you simply play down the bebop scale from those points, but if you descend from the 2nd, 4th, or 6th, a special accommodation must be made to get you back on track with chord tones on the beat. Take a look at the next example. Notice the extra half step when you descend from the 2nd or 6th, and the added notes when you descend from the 4th. While these extra notes are needed to get you back on track, they aren't needed in subsequent octaves if you play further down the scale. In the following example, I descend from each degree of the F7 bebop scale. Keep in mind that this scale can be used over both Cm7 and F7.

TRACK 68

Practice: Play down from all the scale degrees of F7, B♭7, and C7. Throughout this chapter, we will focus on these keys as a preparation for improvising on an F blues. Eventually, you will want to transpose all of this material to all keys.

ARPEGGIOS

Arpeggios are broken chords; the notes are played in succession rather than simultaneously. We can form four-note arpeggios up from any note in the dominant scale, but there are three that are the most common starting points: up from the 3rd, up from the 5th, and up from the 7th.

For an F7 chord, here are three commonly used arpeggios followed by the note that usually comes after each one.

TRACK 69

All of the arpeggios for F7 can also be used with Cm7. There are some tendencies, however. The arpeggio up from the 3rd more clearly suggests F7, and the arpeggio up from the 7th more clearly suggests Cm7. The arpeggio from the 5th uses the notes of Cm7, but if you resolve it to the 3rd of F7, it will sound great over either chord.

The next example shows how the dominant bebop scale can connect to the arpeggios.

TRACK 70

These arpeggios can start on any beat in the measure, so if one starts on beat 4, it will cross the bar line. The following exercise, based on the previous example, gets you used to this and demonstrates how the arpeggios, as well as the scales, work over the iim7 and the V7 chords. You may find that you need to count out loud at first to keep track of the measures.

TRACK 71

Practice: Get comfortable with this exercise and then transpose it to B♭7 and C7 as a preparation for applying this material to the blues in F. Eventually, learn this in all keys. Transposing to all keys will become easier the more you do it. At this point, it's probably very difficult for you. Don't give up hope! Learning to play in all keys is an ongoing process.

Now the fun begins. You can improvise continuous lines using the scales and arpeggios. Each time you land on the 3rd, 5th, or 7th as you descend the bebop scale, decide whether you want to go up an arpeggio or continue descending the scale. Notice that two of the arpeggios can be used to lead into other arpeggios.

Here is an example of what your dominant bebop scale improvisation might sound like.

TRACK 72

Practice: Improvise your own continuous lines using the dominant bebop scale and arpeggios. After you are comfortable creating right-hand lines, add the chords with the left hand. Start with this key and then work on C7 and Bb7 before moving on to the other keys.

RESOLUTION TO THE THIRD

Here is an idea that I call "resolution to the third." It is really just a fancy way of moving from the 4th degree of the dominant scale to the 3rd.

TRACK 73

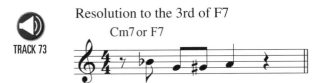

It can be inserted into the dominant scale.

TRACK 74

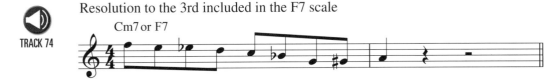

It can also be included at the top of an arpeggio from the 5th.

TRACK 75

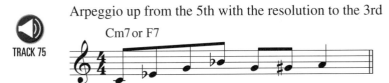

Here is how I might include the resolution to the 3rd idea in a line.

TRACK 76

Practice: Include the resolution to the 3rd idea in your dominant scale improvisations.

APPLICATION TO THE BLUES

It's time to apply all of this new vocabulary to the blues. We will begin by playing individual bebop scale segments over each chord of a blues in F. In the following example, I play down from the second degree of each scale.

Practice: Learn to play scale segments down from all scale degrees on the F blues. For example, play a whole chorus descending from the root of each chord, then a whole chorus descending from the second degree of each scale (as in the example above), then a whole chorus descending from the third degree of each scale, and so on.

Next, we will play arpeggios on the blues. In this example, I play arpeggios up from the 3rd of each chord. In some cases, to give the line a more syncopated jazz feel, I have added two notes after the arpeggio so that the phrase ends on an upbeat.

Practice: Get comfortable with the example above and then try using the arpeggios that start on the 5th and 7th.

When you hear a good improvisation, you will notice that the line doesn't necessarily stop when moving from one chord to the next; it often continues on through. Achieving a command of scales will allow you to move seamlessly through a series of chord changes. The following example shows you ways of making scale connections and will prepare you to use bebop scales on the F blues. In some cases, I have either left out the passing tone or put in an additional passing tone right before the chord change to ensure a smooth transition. I marked these spots with either NPT for "no passing tone" or APT for "additional passing tone." I also show you how the resolution to the 3rd idea can be used to connect to a new chord in the next measure. In several spots (measure 17 leading into 18, measure 19 leading into 20, measure 31 leading into 32, and measure 33 leading into 34), I used a slightly different type of connection. I played a note a half step above and then a note a half step below the chord tone I wanted to land on. This is an example of a technique called **enclosure**.

There are many ways these scale connections can be done. In many cases, there are multiple solutions that would be effective. Study these examples to gain a general understanding of how to connect.

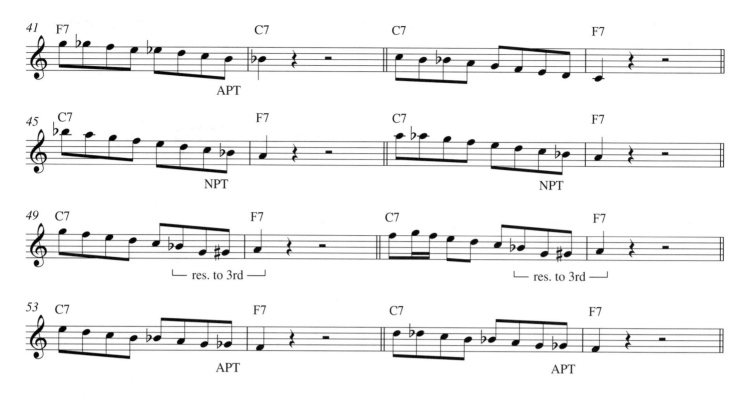

Up to this point, the scale connection examples have involved scales that lead to a chord tone. In many cases, however, scales will lead you to non-chord tones. If you land on the second, fourth, or sixth degree of a dominant scale, you can use the techniques described earlier to get you back on track with chord tones on the beat. In the following example, I land on the 2nd of the Bb7 scale.

TRACK 80

Here I land on the 4th of the C7 scale.

TRACK 81

Here I land on the 6th of the F7 scale.

TRACK 82

Here is an example of how you can play long, connected lines on the F blues using much of the dominant material I have introduced thus far.

Practice: Create your own lines in this same manner.

MORE DOMINANT IDEAS

Here are a few more ideas you can incorporate into your lines.

The next example shows how you can play inverted arpeggios from the 3rd and 7th. It is possible to invert an arpeggio from the 5th, but this was rarely done by Charlie Parker and the other bebop masters.

Here is an example of what it can sound like when I string all of this together.

TRACK 86

Practice: Play the example above and then transpose this line into B♭7 and C7. Practice your own ways of stringing ideas together in these keys, then move on to the other keys. Getting this material together in all 12 keys will take a long time, so this can be an ongoing project as you continue to work on other things. This is when a practice log comes in handy to keep track of exercises you have practiced, keys you have mastered, and tempos you have become comfortable with. It will help you track your progress and set goals. Continue to use a metronome and/or backing tracks.

MORE ABOUT ACCENTS

We talked before about adding accents on the upbeats of a series of eighth notes. This is usually where accents are added if a line is moving in one direction, either ascending or descending; however, there is quite a bit more variation that can occur. The highest pitched points of a line often receive strong accents. These can occur on the beat or on the upbeat. Perhaps, not by accident, language is similar in this regard. Say any multisyllabic word – "multisyllabic," for example. Notice that the highest pitched syllable "lab" gets the accent. This is just one more way in which jazz melody is linked to speech. In addition, the first note of a phrase usually gets an accent. Certain target notes, notes the line is headed toward, sometimes get accented as well. When an accent falls on the beat, we don't typically accent on the upbeat immediately before or after. If you have the technology to slow down a solo by a great jazz pianist or a horn player such as Charlie Parker, it will be easier to analyze where accents occur.

The following example shows what I come up with if I apply these accent "rules" to the line from the previous example.

In reality, however, it may not feel natural to include all of these accents, and some may be stronger than others. There is not one absolute or correct way to apply them. It is up to the individual player.

RHYTHMIC VARIATIONS

Although eighth notes are the basic note value of many jazz solos, there is no end to the rhythmic variety that can be incorporated. One basic way to add syncopation is to begin a scale on an upbeat. You can think of the starting note as a pickup into the next note. Descend from the second note in a way that is appropriate for that scale degree.

Here is the F7 bebop scale descending from all scale degrees, beginning on an upbeat. In the following examples, I begin the phrase on the "and" of 1, but you can begin these phrases on the "and" of any beat in the measure.

You can include an additional note so that a scale, or any phrase for that matter, ends on an upbeat.

You can also vary the rhythm of the arpeggios. Here are some good ways to begin a phrase. These arpeggios start on an upbeat followed by a triplet.

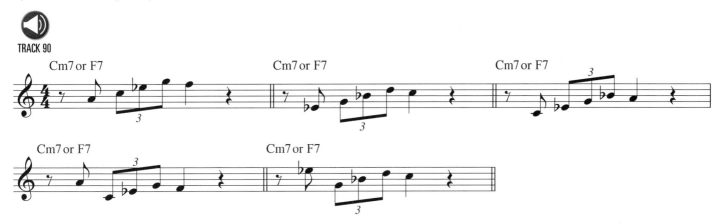

Here are some more ways to begin a phrase. The top note of the arpeggio is now on the beat, affecting how you continue down the scale. These arpeggios start on an upbeat – without a triplet.

Here are some more good ways to include a triplet with an arpeggio. Starting the arpeggio on beat 1 or beat 3 will sound the best.

TRACK 92

You can begin an arpeggio with a triplet. Again, because the top note of the arpeggio is now on the beat, the way you come down the scale is affected. Start the arpeggio on any beat in the measure.

TRACK 93

PHRASING

A good solo unfolds like someone telling a story; there are highs and lows, suspenseful moments, and sudden outbursts. Phrasing plays a large role in setting up this drama. Many solos start with short phrases that draw the listener in, eventually incorporating longer, more complex phrases that sustain the listener's interest. Phrases can be of any length and can begin and end on any beat, just like the variety of sentences we hear when people are conversing. Listen to classic solos and take notice of where the rests occur that set off the phrases. Sometimes these rests occur at the end of a musical idea, like a pause after a period at the end of a sentence. Sometimes… rests or pauses… occur in the middle… of a musical strain. Suspense is created when the line pauses………. and relief is felt when it continues on.

The following examples show how a continuous line can be broken up to create more interest.

Let's start with this continuous line.

TRACK 94

Here's how I might break up the line by adding pauses.

TRACK 95

In the following example, I've broken it up in a different way, using the same series of notes.

TRACK 96

Here is the same series of notes broken up in yet another way.

TRACK 97

Practice: Incorporate rhythmic variations and this type of phrasing into your improvisations.

Here is an example of an F blues solo that includes many of the techniques discussed in this chapter.

TRACK 98

Practice: This chapter has provided you with a lot of vocabulary. Become proficient using this material on an F blues. Then work on improvising on the blues in C and B♭. Work toward being able to play all of this dominant vocabulary in all keys.

Chapter 7

MAJOR VOCABULARY

MAJOR SCALE IMPROVISATION

The previous chapter provided you with techniques for improvising over dominant 7th chords and, as you learned, this material also works over a iim7–V7 progression. For example, you can use G7 material over Dm7 and G7 because they form a iim7–V7 progression. Many tunes make use of the iim7–V7–Imaj7 progression. Now's the time to explore ways of improvising over Imaj7. The concepts you learned in the previous chapter regarding phrasing and accents will be applicable here as well.

The major scale, sometimes referred to as the Ionian mode, is the scale that we most often use when improvising over major 7th chords. As in the case of the Mixolydian mode, the fourth note of this scale is a weak tone. For example, if you play an E♭ in your right hand against a B♭maj7 in your left, you will hear the "clash" and feel the need for this note to resolve. Keep this in mind as you improvise melodies using the major scale. Here is an example of what an improvisation with the B♭ major scale can sound like.

TRACK 99

THE MAJOR BEBOP SCALE

A major bebop scale can be created by adding a passing tone between the fifth and sixth degrees of a major scale. It is most often played descending. The added passing tone (the ♭6th) positions the chord tones of a major 6th chord on the beats of the measure and the weak tone (the 4th) on an upbeat. You can play this scale over a major 6th or a major 7th chord.

Here is the descending B♭ major bebop scale.

TRACK 100

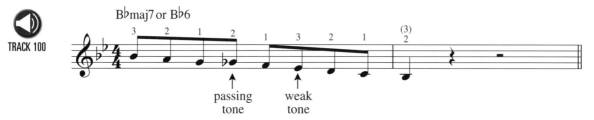

Practice: Learn to play the major bebop scale in all keys. With each scale, play a major 7th chord or major 6th chord with the left hand. Use the fingerings in parentheses if you want to continue further down the scale.

TRACK 101

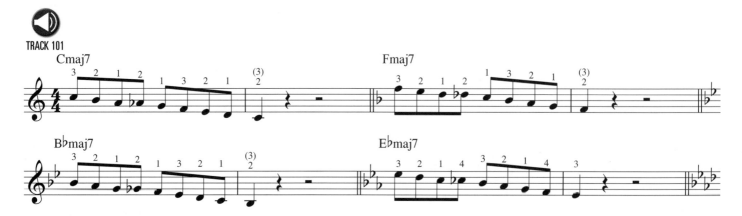

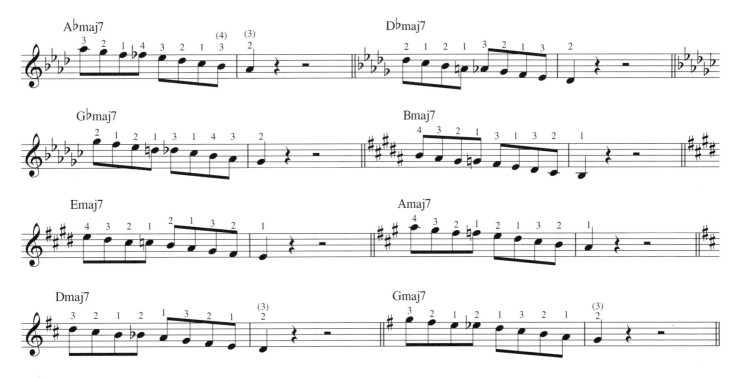

Now, learn to play down from any note in the major bebop scale (other than from the passing tone between the 5th and 6th). If you descend from the tonic, 3rd, 5th, or 6th, you simply play down the major bebop scale from these points, but if you descend from the 2nd, 4th, or 7th, you need to make a special accommodation to get you back on track, i.e., to position the notes of a major 6th chord on the beat. Notice the extra half step when you descend from the 2nd or 7th and the added notes when you descend from the 4th. These extra notes get you back on track, and aren't needed in subsequent octaves if you play further down the scale. Here's the B♭ major bebop scale descending from all scale degrees.

TRACK 102

Practice: Play down from all the scale degrees of B♭ major, A♭ major, and C major. Throughout this chapter, we will focus on these keys as preparation for later exercises. Eventually, you will want to transpose to all keys.

RESOLUTION TO THE THIRD AND FIFTH

You can insert the resolution to the 3rd idea into the major bebop scale.

TRACK 103

└ resolution to the 3rd ┘

It also works to include a resolution to the 5th.

TRACK 104

└ resolution to the 5th ┘

ARPEGGIOS AND OTHER MELODIC IDEAS

Play an arpeggio up from the 3rd and connect to the scale.

TRACK 105

└ arpeggio from the 3rd ┘

Play an inverted arpeggio from the 3rd and connect to the scale.

TRACK 106

└ inverted arpeggio ┘
from the 3rd

Here are some more ideas that can be connected to the scale.

TRACK 107

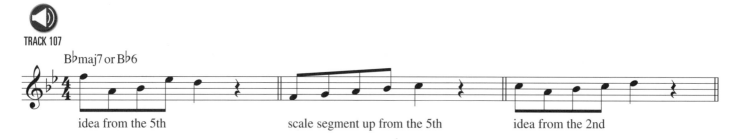

idea from the 5th　　　　scale segment up from the 5th　　　　idea from the 2nd

Sometimes, the idea from the 5th is combined with the resolution to the 3rd idea.

TRACK 108

Here is an example of what it can sound like when I string all of these ideas together.

TRACK 109

Practice: Play the example above and then transpose this line into A♭ major and C major. Practice your own ways of stringing ideas together in these keys, then move on to the other keys.

RHYTHMIC VARIATIONS

You can start scales, arpeggios, and other ideas on upbeats, just as you did with the dominant material. You can include triplets with the arpeggio from the 3rd. You can also add a note if you want to end a phrase on an upbeat. Here are some examples of major phrases with rhythmic variations.

TRACK 110

Practice: Incorporate these rhythmic variations as you continue to work on stringing together major material.

IMPROVISING OVER COMMON PROGRESSIONS

Now let's apply this material to the iim7–V7–Imaj7 progression. Begin by playing down a dominant bebop scale over the iim7–V7 measure and continue in the major 7th measure using major scale vocabulary. In the following example, I start on each degree of the F7 scale and make a smooth connection into the next measure. I use connections similar to those I showed you on page 45 (Track 79) in Chapter 6.

TRACK 111

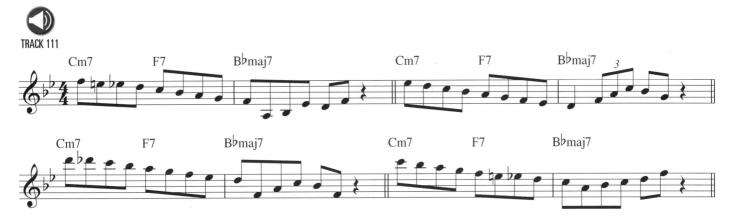

Next, add some dominant arpeggios and other ideas into the iim7–V7 measures.

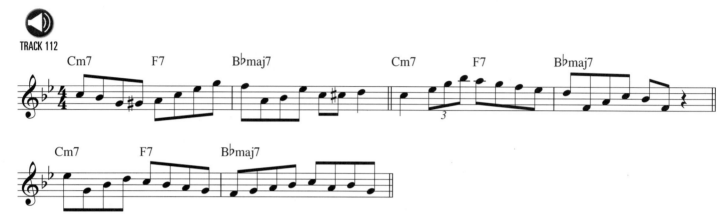

Another common chord progression is Imaj7–vim7–iim7–V7. It is often used as a **turnaround**, a progression that leads back to the beginning of a section or to the top of a tune. This progression or variations of it are the basis for entire sections – the A sections of "Blue Moon" by Richard Rodgers, for example. The entire tune "Nutty" by Thelonious Monk is based on variations of this progression.

To improvise over the vim7 chord, you can simply play the major scale or major bebop scale based on the Imaj7 because these two chords are so similar in sound and function. This means that you can improvise over this progression using just two scales, the major bebop scale over the Imaj7 and the vim7, and a dominant bebop scale over the iim7 and the V7.

A common variation of this progression is to play iiim7–vim7–iim7–V7. The iiim7 is closely related in sound and function to the Imaj7. Improvise over iiim7 with a major scale or major bebop scale as if it were Imaj7. Play the example below to learn how you can connect these two scales. Notice how I sometimes left out the passing tone or put in an additional passing tone right before a chord change to ensure a smooth transition from one scale to the next. Here, the bebop scales are applied to the Imaj7–vim7–iim7–V7 and iiim7–vim7–iim7–V7 progressions.

Now, if you add in all of your major and dominant licks to the mix, you'll be able to form some very cool sounding lines. Here's an improvisation over Imaj7–vim7–iim7–V7 and iiim7–vim7–iim7–V7 that demonstrates what this can sound like.

TRACK 114

The next example is an improvisation over Imaj7–vim7–iim7–V7 and iiim7–vim7–iim7–V7, this time in the key of C, with one chord per measure.

TRACK 115

Practice: Learn to improvise lines over Imaj7–vim7–iim7–V7 and iiim7–vim7–iim7–V7 using the dominant and major vocabulary I have shown you.

APPLICATION TO "Afternoon in Paris"

"Afternoon in Paris" by John Lewis is a 32-measure tune with an AABA form. It is ideal for practicing what we have covered so far. The A sections make use of the iim7–V7–Imaj7 progression in three keys (C, B♭, and A♭). The bridge begins in the key of C with a iim7–V7 that leads into Imaj7–vim7–iim7–V7, followed by C♯m7–F♯7, a iim7–V7, over which I play F♯7 bebop scale material, and finally Dm7–G7, a iim7–V7, that leads to the last A section.

Here is an example of a solo on the chord progression of "Afternoon in Paris" that makes use of many of the techniques you have learned about so far.

TRACK 116

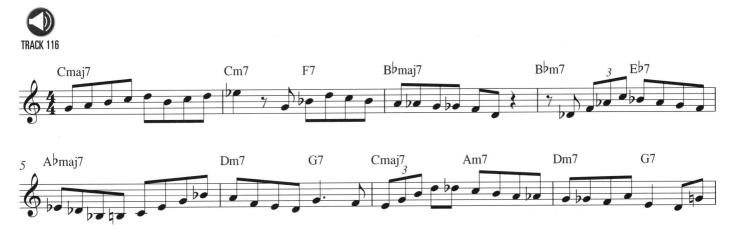

Practice: Learn to play the melody of "Afternoon in Paris" from a fake book or figure it out by ear from a recording. Improvise your own solos using all of the vocabulary you have been learning. Remember, it is okay to work things out. Composing a solo is a great way to get familiar with vocabulary. Create a complete performance of this tune by playing the head, followed by as many choruses of improvisation as you like. After your solo, play the head again to end the tune.

Chapter 8

MORE HARMONY

UPPER EXTENSIONS

Upper extensions are notes that can be added to chords. They provide color and complexity and are a hallmark of jazz harmony. You can add up to three extensions to most 7th chords, but not all of them are appropriate in every situation. Knowing which extensions are suitable requires an understanding of the harmonic context and, often, simply using your ears as a guide. When you create voicings, you can pick and choose which extensions you want to include. And you can scramble up the order of the notes in all sorts of ways to come up with an incredible variety of effective voicings. The chart below shows the upper extension formulas for six basic 7th chords.

Major 7th	9	#11	13		Half-diminished 7th	9	11	♭13	
Dominant 7th	9	#11	13		Diminished 7th	9	11	♭13	maj7
Minor 7th	9	11	13		Minor-major 7th	9	11	13	

In their basic position, the upper extensions of each chord form a triad that is an octave plus a whole step higher than what I call the "underlying triad" (the root, 3rd, and 5th of the chord). For example, the extensions for Cmaj7 are D, F♯, and A, which form a D major triad. (See the example that follows.) These three extensions are an octave plus a whole step higher than the underlying triad (C, E, and G in this case). When the underlying triad is minor, the upper extensions form a minor triad an octave plus a whole step above it. When the underlying triad is diminished, the upper extensions form a diminished triad an octave plus a whole step above.

The extensions are assigned numbers based on the major scale. As you play up a major scale, it is useful to note that the 9th, 11th, and 13th degrees are the same notes, but an octave higher than the 2nd, 4th, and 6th, respectively. This can help you think of these upper extensions more easily, and chord symbols sometimes make use of the smaller number equivalents. In addition, the #11th is sometimes referred to as the ♭5th.

The diminished 7th chord is unique because you can add four upper extensions to it. Its upper extensions form a diminished 7th chord an octave plus a whole step above. The extensions of the diminished 7th are the 9th, 11th, ♭13th, and major 7th. You might think to call this last extension by a larger number, but it is usually described as the major 7th (maj7 or ∆7) when included in a chord symbol.

Here is an example of these chords and extensions with C as the root of each chord. The 7th chords are in the left hand, with extensions in the right hand.

TRACK 117

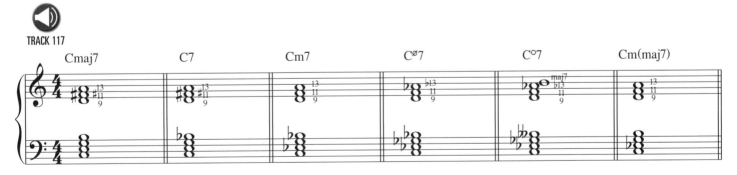

Practice: Play a chord with the left hand and the upper extensions with the right, as in the example above. Do this with the six chord qualities in all 12 keys.

Sometimes, chord symbols use an extension in place of the 7th. In these cases, the 7th is still played, as well as the extension indicated. For example, Fm9 is Fm7 with the 9th added, Dm11 is Dm7 with the 11th added, and B♭13 is a B♭7 with the 13th added. Sometimes a chord symbol contains several extensions. Often, chord symbols are intended to be just a guide or suggestion. Jazz pianists routinely add extensions that are not indicated on a chart to get the sound they desire.

ALTERED DOMINANT EXTENSIONS

When it comes to adding extensions, dominant chords have the most possibilities. This is because, in addition to the 9th, #11th, and 13th, there are three more extensions that can be used to add more tension and urgency to the sound of a dominant 7th chord: ♭9th, #9th, and ♭13th. These three tones, along with the #11, are known as **altered dominant tones** or **altered dominant extensions**.

You will encounter a variety of symbols when dealing with altered dominant extensions. The symbol #9 and the symbol +9 mean the same thing. ♭13 can be written as ♭5 or +5. C+7 means C7#5, which can also be written as C7(+5) or C7♭13. C7alt generally means to include one or more of the following: ♭9th, #9th, ♭13th. C7alt can also include the #11th. When the #11th is included in the C7alt, it is most often used in combination with one or more of the other altered extensions.

While the six extensions that can be added to a dominant chord (9th, ♭9th, #9th, #11th, 13th, ♭13th) can be combined in many ways, an altered 9th is not typically paired with an unaltered 9th, and the ♭13th is not usually paired with the unaltered 13th. When the ♭13 is used, the 5th of the chord is generally left out. The #11th can be combined with any of the other extensions.

Here are the ♭9th, #9th, and ♭13th applied to a C7 chord.

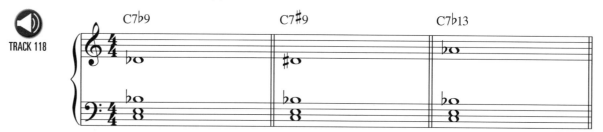

Practice: Play the example above and take it around the cycle (transpose it to the other keys in the cycle).

TWO-HANDED VOICINGS

Voicings used for comping or to harmonize a melody often include extensions. So far, you have practiced the extensions in their basic position, but when creating voicings, they can be placed in different octaves and rearranged in all sorts of ways. To create full-sounding chords, we often play voicings that require two hands. Here are some suggestions of how to get started using the right hand to add another note to the shell voicings.

With closed-shell voicings, add the 9th. You may choose, as I have in this example, to retain the ♭5th with the half-diminished and diminished 7th chords since this note helps differentiate them from other chord qualities.

With closed-shell dominant chords you have more options; you can add the 9th, ♭9th, or #9th.

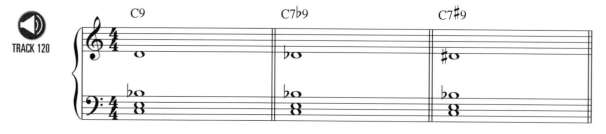

With open-shell voicings, add the 5th on top. On dominant chords, however, it is more common to add the 13th or ♭13th instead of the 5th. The following example demonstrates open-shell voicings with one note added.

The next four examples offer suggestions for adding two notes to the shell voicings. With closed-shell voicings, except for half-diminished and diminished 7th, you can add the 9th and the 5th with the right hand. In the case of half-diminished and diminished 7th, I retained the ♭5th in the left hand and added the 9th and 11th with the right.

TRACK 122

Combining the 9th, ♭9th, or ♯9th with the 5th on closed-shell dominant chords is possible, but using the 13th or ♭13th in lieu of the 5th will provide more harmonic color. (I didn't include the combinations ♯9th and 13th or 9th and ♭13th because they are used less often.) The following example demonstrates some of these possibilities.

TRACK 123

With open-shell voicings, you can add the 5th and the 9th with the right hand, but in the case of the dominant 7th chords, I again added the 13th or ♭13th instead of the 5th and used one or the other in combination with the 9th, ♭9th, or ♯9th. As before, I didn't include the combinations ♯9th and 13th or 9th and ♭13th on the dominant 7th because they are used less often. In the second major 7th voicing, I used the 13th (6th) instead of the 5th. I also included a useful half-diminished voicing and diminished 7th voicing that make use of the root in place of the 9th. Note the different positions of the 9th and altered 9th throughout.

TRACK 124

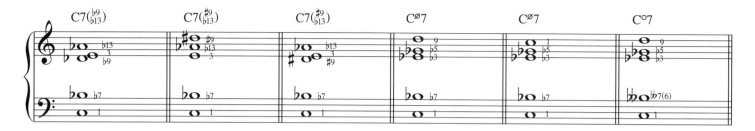

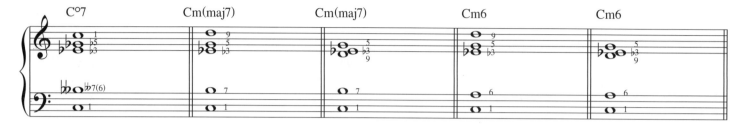

Using these suggestions, here's how I might play Imaj7–vim7–iim7–V7.

TRACK 125

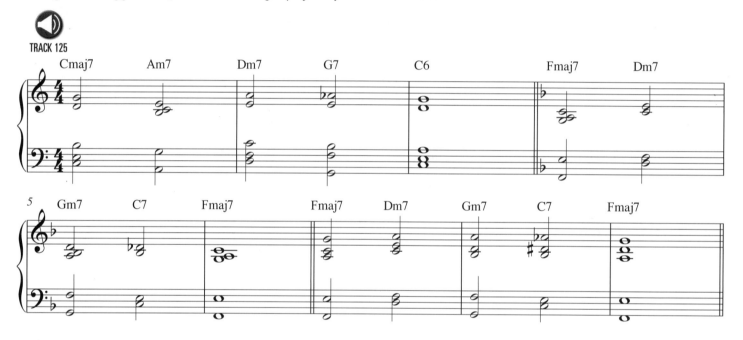

Practice: Learn to play Imaj7–vim7–iim7–V7 in other keys. Start with common keys like G, C, F, B♭, and E♭ before transposing to those further afield.

HARMONIZING TUNES

When you add extensions to harmonize a tune, make sure you pick notes that are compatible with the melody. Also, since we tend to hear the top note of a voicing as the melody, keep the notes you add below the desired melody. Decide which chords will be open and which will be closed before you begin adding extensions. At first, you will probably think of harmony in a strictly vertical sense, as if each voicing stands on its own. However, you must also consider the horizontal movement of the individual notes within each voicing as you move from one chord to the next. This will help you determine which extensions to use and which voicings are most appropriate.

Here is an example of how you might use shell voicings and extensions to harmonize the tune "Poor Butterfly." You can play the top note of the open-shell voicings with your right-hand thumb or play broken chords. In measure 27, I decided to play just the bass note rather than a whole chord because of what is going on in the melody. Sometimes a melody note may coincide with the top note of a chord voicing. This is the case in measure 25, so I left off the top D♭ from the B♭m7 open-shell voicing and instead played that note with the right hand as part of the melody.

It is common, albeit optional, to add one or more altered extensions to a dominant 7th chord that leads to a chord of any quality that is up a 4th or down a 5th (as in measure 18 of "Poor Butterfly" below). But if this chord you are leading to is minor, extensions added are usually altered (as in the G7 leading to Cm7 in Track 135, page 68). Analyze which extensions I have added in this example. In measure 30, you will find I added the #11th on E♭7.

POOR BUTTERFLY

Words by John L. Golden
Music by Raymond Hubbell

TRACK 126

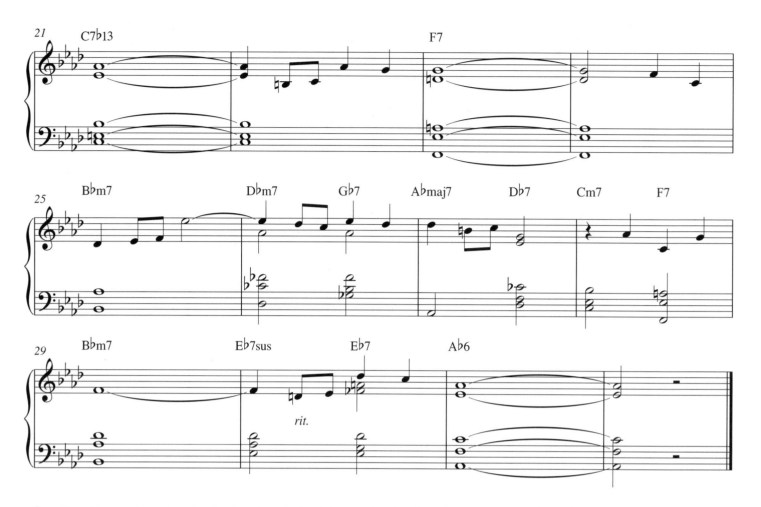

Practice: Harmonize other standards using shell voicings and extensions. Use the suggestions above to get started, but don't be afraid to experiment with other possibilities. You can try adding other extensions such as the 11th and ♯11th.

ROOTLESS VOICINGS

In the 1950s, pianists such as Bill Evans and Red Garland began using middle-register, **rootless voicings**. This has become a popular way to play the left hand, especially in a group setting with a bassist to supply the roots. There are two basic ways to play each chord quality using this technique: one similar to the closed shell, in that the 3rd is below the 7th (non-inverted), and the other like the open shell, in that the 7th is below the 3rd (inverted). Below are formulas for some of the most common four-note rootless voicings. The numbers correspond to notes of a major scale. Jazz pianists sometimes leave out the second-to-lowest note to create three-note rootless voicings, or even play just the 3rd and 7th, or 7th and 3rd of each chord to create two-note rootless voicings.

Rootless Voicing Formulas

	Non-inverted				Inverted			
Major 7th	3	5	7	9	7	9	3	5
Major 6th	3	5	6	9	6	9	3	5
Minor 7th	♭3	5	♭7	9	♭7	9	♭3	5
Dominant 7th	3	13	♭7	9	♭7	9	3	13
Altered Dominant	3	♭13	♭7	♯9	♭7	♯9	3	♭13
	3	13	♭7	♭9	♭7	♭9	3	13
	3	5	♭7	♭9	♭7	♭9	3	5
Half-diminished	♭3	♭5	♭7	1	♭7	1	♭3	♭5
	♭3	♭5	♭7	9	♭7	9	♭3	♭5
Diminished 7th	1	♭3	♭5	♭♭7 (or any inversion of this)				
Minor-major 7th	♭3	5	7	9	7	9	♭3	5
Minor 6th	♭3	5	6	9	6	9	♭3	5

Here are these formulas shown in musical notation.

TRACK 127

Practice: Learn to play each voicing in all keys through the cycle using the left hand. I usually play the voicings as low as possible without any of the notes going below the C an octave below middle C. For practice purposes, you may want to hold the sustain pedal down as you play the root followed by the rootless voicing. This will allow you to hear what it will sound like when you have a bass player. Make sure you clear the pedal when you move to the next chord. When playing with a bassist, it isn't necessary to play the roots.

In the following example, I use the non-inverted major 7th rootless voicing to demonstrate how you might practice.

TRACK 128

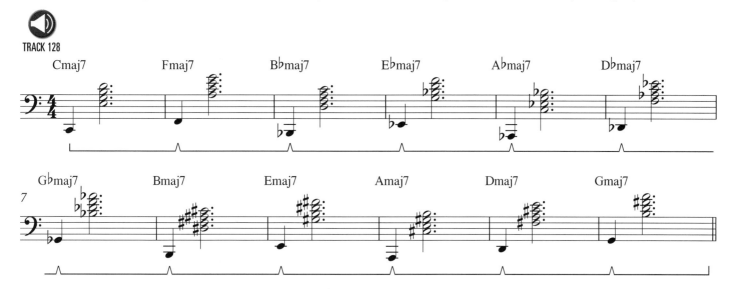

When you use rootless voicings in a tune, it is important, just as it is with shell voicings, to achieve smooth voice leading. In the following example, I play through the cycle alternating between non-inverted and inverted major 7th rootless voicings. I show these voicings in their ideal range. A♭maj7 can be played high or low.

TRACK 129

Here are the rootless major 7th voicings played a different way. Chords that were inverted in the previous example are non-inverted here, and those that were non-inverted are inverted. These voicings are shown in their ideal range. Dmaj7 can be played high or low.

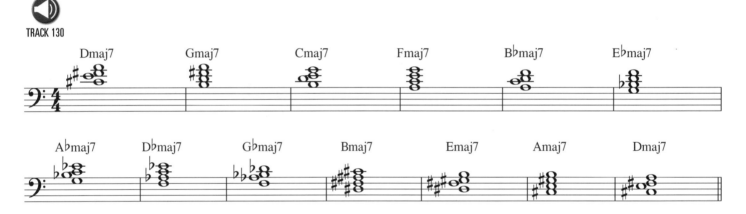

TRACK 130

Practice: Once you are comfortable alternating between inverted and non-inverted major 7th rootless voicings, do the same for minor 7th and dominant 7th chords.

The following example shows two ways I use rootless voicings to play iim7–V7–Imaj7. Notice that the smoothest voice leading occurs by alternating between inverted and non-inverted.

TRACK 131

Practice: Play iim7–V7–Imaj7 with rootless voicings in all keys. Alternate between inverted and non-inverted.

The next example shows two ways I use rootless voicings to play Imaj7–vim7–iim7–V7. Again, the smoothest voice leading occurs by alternating between inverted and non-inverted.

TRACK 132

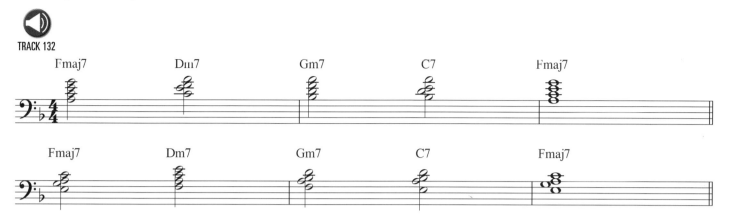

Practice: Play Imaj7–vim7–iim7–V7 with rootless voicings in all keys. Alternate between inverted and non-inverted.

Try using an altered dominant rootless voicing for the V7 chord.

TRACK 133

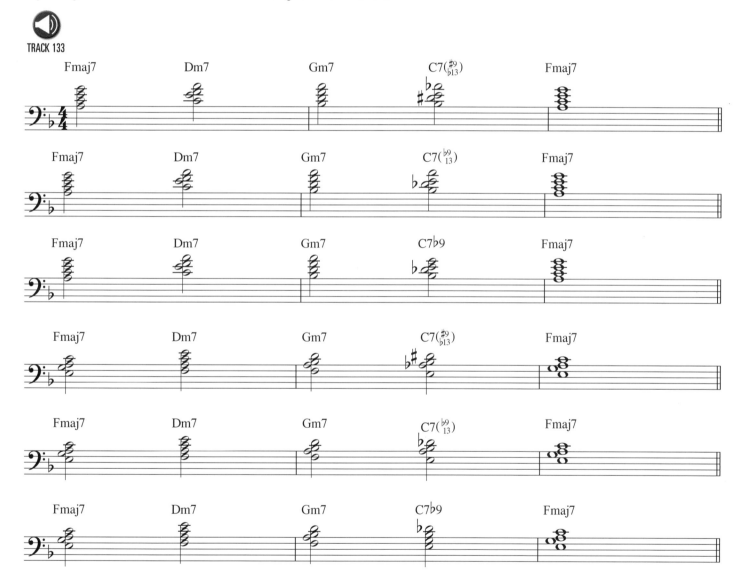

Because iiim7 is so closely related in sound and function to the Imaj7, use the Imaj7 rootless voicing for both. In the following example of iiim7–vim7–iim7–V7 played with rootless voicings, I use the same voicing for both Dm7 (iiim7) and the B♭maj7 (Imaj7) that follows.

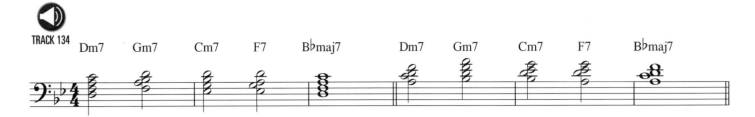

TRACK 134

It is common to play an altered dominant in place of the vim7 to lead to the iim7. Try playing Imaj7–VI7alt–iim7–V7. Here is that progression with rootless voicings.

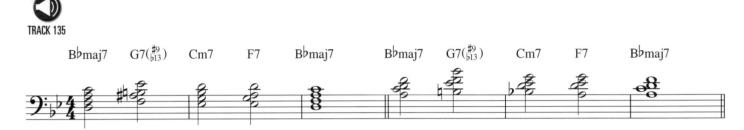

TRACK 135

Practice: Learn to play the three previous examples in all keys. Mastering all these voicings is a big project. Start with the keys that are most familiar to you. Use your practice log to keep track of the keys you know and which ones you still need to learn.

Here is the tune "Indiana (Back Home Again in Indiana)" played with rootless voicings. In the process of applying rootless voicings, it is important, as it is with shell voicings, to find a good balance of smooth voice leading and chords that are in an ideal register.

TRACK 136

INDIANA
(Back Home Again in Indiana)

Words by Ballard MacDonald
Music by James F. Hanley

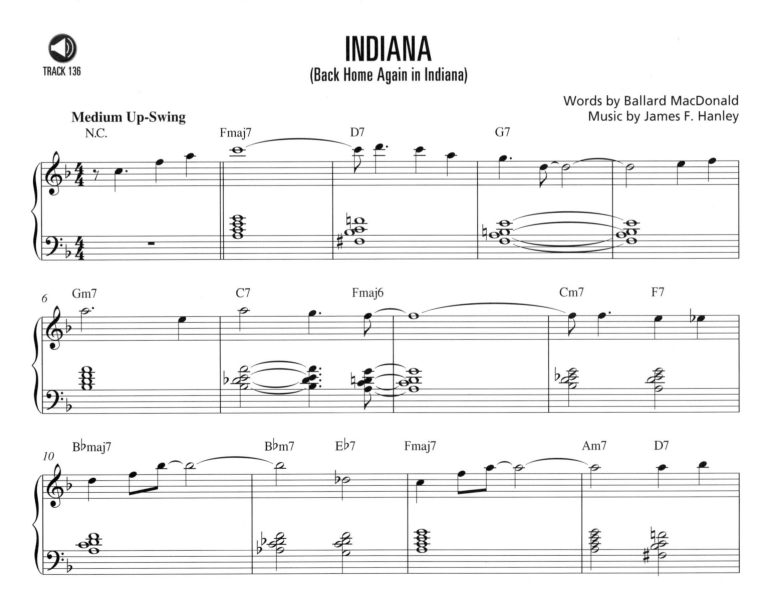

Practice: Apply rootless voicings to other standards you know or are learning.

COMPING RHYTHMS

Whether comping with the left hand to support your right-hand lines, or comping with two hands behind a soloist, you can play rhythms that will drive the music forward, add interest, and even create a dialog between the solo and the accompaniment. Let's take a look at how this can be done.

When we comp, we sometimes anticipate chords by an eighth note. This means that if a chord change happens on beat 1, we might actually play the chord on the "and" of 4 of the preceding measure, or if a chord change happens on beat 3, we might play the chord on the "and" of 2. Red Garland often comped consistently on the "and" of 2 and the "and" of 4.

Here is an example of this left-hand comping rhythm with a right-hand improvisation.

You may have noticed that I left off the top note of the final F7 voicing in the example above (measure 8). I did this because the right-hand melody dipped down lower at that point. When you improvise, you can leave out upper notes of your left-hand voicings to accommodate the right hand. Sometimes you might switch to a shell voicing momentarily, or leave the left hand out entirely to allow for lower notes in the right hand.

Practice: Use the left-hand comping rhythm from the example above while you play basic scales or improvise solos with your right hand.

When you comp with the left hand for your own solos or comp with two hands behind a soloist, the "Red Garland rhythm" is one option, but you can also vary whether you play the chords on the beat or on an upbeat, and whether you play them short or long. Comping rhythms can coincide with the rhythm of the solo, or they can be used to fill in the spaces between melodic phrases, creating an exchange or dialog. Pianists sometimes **lay out** (stop playing) behind a soloist for one or more sections or even one or more choruses.

Here is an example of a solo on a B♭ blues accompanied by left-hand chords that use these rhythmic techniques.

Practice: Improvise on the blues and other tunes and vary your left-hand comping rhythms.

COMPING BEHIND A SOLOIST

When comping behind a soloist, you need to do your best to make the whole band groove *and* make the soloist sound good. If you do that, *you* will sound good! Support, but don't overwhelm, the soloist. We customarily use two-handed voicings. They can be created from shell voicings and extensions, as I showed you earlier, or they can be based on rootless voicings. One technique is to move the second-to-lowest note of a rootless voicing up an octave. The notes of the voicing that result can be divided between the hands however you like.

Here is an example based on the first 16 bars of "Indiana (Back Home Again in Indiana)."

TRACK 139

You can use the right hand to add one or more notes to the rootless voicings to create all kinds of possibilities. With your right hand drawing upon the same scales you use when you improvise, add either a single note or an octave above the left-hand rootless voicings. Remember, you can play four-note, three-note, or two-note rootless voicings. Play both hands at the same time to create full-sounding chords. Here is an example of two-handed comping on the blues.

TRACK 140

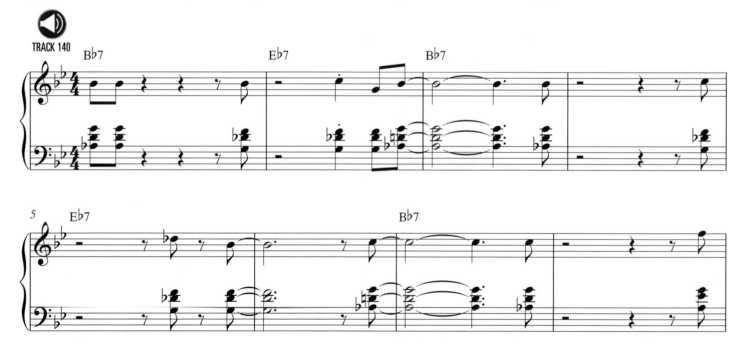

Practice: Comp on the blues and other tunes using the techniques described above.

SOLOING WITH CHORDS

Two-handed voicings are essential for comping, but they can also be used for soloing. Pianists sometimes begin their solos with single-note lines that eventually give way to two-handed chords that help build energy and excitement. Bobby Timmons's solo on "Moanin'" with Art Blakey is a classic example of this. Adding a perfect 4th below the upper note of a right-hand octave is a technique Red Garland often used to "fatten up" his chords. Here is an example of a solo in that style.

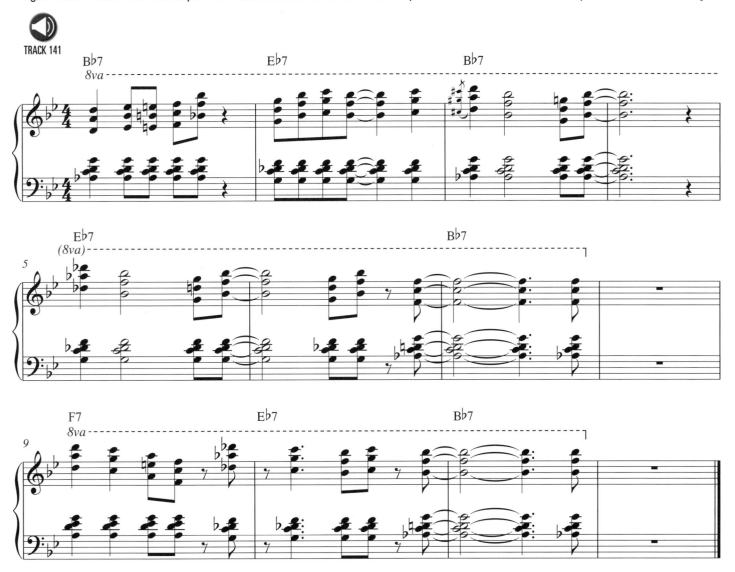

Practice: Work on improvising with two-handed chords on the blues or other tunes. Play both hands at the same time to create big chords. Try beginning your solos with single-note lines and then change to chords toward the end to build excitement.

Chapter 9
MORE SCALES

THE HARMONIC MINOR SCALE

The **harmonic minor scale** is like a major scale, but with the third and sixth degrees flatted. You can also view it as an Aeolian mode (natural minor scale) with a raised seventh degree. Here is the F harmonic minor scale.

TRACK 142

THE JEWISH OR SPANISH SCALE

In Chapter 5, I showed you how to use the Mixolydian mode to improvise over dominant chords and in Chapter 6, I introduced you to the dominant bebop scale. When we improvise over an altered dominant chord, however, a different scale is required. Often, we use the fifth mode of the harmonic minor scale. This mode is known as the **Jewish scale** or **Spanish scale**. If I play the fifth mode of F harmonic minor, I get the C7 Jewish scale. The following example shows this scale and how its notes relate to C7.

TRACK 143

The Jewish scale is like a Mixolydian mode, but with a lowered 2nd (♭9th) and a lowered 6th (♭13th). The fourth note of the scale (labeled above as the 11th) is a weak tone. The Jewish scale is frequently used to lead to a chord of any quality that is up a 4th or down a 5th, but most often, this scale precedes a minor chord.

Dominant voicings used in conjunction with the Jewish scale often include the ♭9th. They might also include the ♯9th, although this note is not contained within the scale, so it does not precisely match the harmonic sound of the scale. The ♭13th can be incorporated as well – although, depending on the melodic line, it is sometimes best to omit this note, or use the 5th instead. These voicings should not involve the 9th, ♯11th, or 13th.

We can form a descending bebop version of the Jewish scale by adding the major 7th as a passing tone. The following example shows how I can play down from any degree in the scale (other than from the passing tone (the major 7th)) and lead into a minor chord. In some cases, I have made an adjustment in order to land on a chord tone of the minor chord.

TRACK 144

Practice: Learn to play the scale connections above and transpose them to G7 and D7 as preparation for exercises and tunes we will explore later.

You can play an arpeggio from the 3rd of the Jewish scale. It forms a diminished arpeggio and can be played ascending or inverted. These arpeggios can be followed by a continuation of the Jewish scale or they can be used to lead to a note in the next chord.

You can play a resolution to the 5th, a resolution to the 3rd, or a resolution to the root.

You can combine the arpeggio or inverted arpeggio with the resolution to the root.

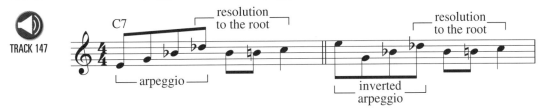

Sometimes the resolution to the root can instead be used to lead to a note in the next chord. Notice the difference in the two phrases in the following example. In the second phrase, I moved the end of the line up an octave. This is a common bebop lick.

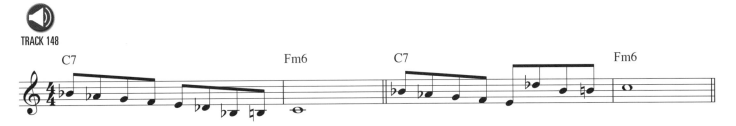

Practice: Learn to play these Jewish scale ideas and transpose them to G7 and D7. Eventually, you will want to transpose all of the Jewish scale material to all keys.

MINOR II–V–I

If you recall, the major scale was the source for the iim7–V7–Imaj7 progression. We can generate a progression in similar fashion from the harmonic minor scale. The result is known as a minor II–V–I.

II–V–I in F minor

Notice that all of the notes in the chords above come from the F harmonic minor scale. The V7 chord has been extended to include the ♭9th. The example shows the progression in its basic form, however, different combinations of altered tones can be used over the V7, and the im(maj7) is often replaced with im6 or im7. Jazz musicians generally improvise with a different scale over each chord of this progression. Let's take a look at what those scales are.

THE LOCRIAN MODE

The **Locrian mode** is the seventh mode of the major scale, and it is often the best choice to use when improvising over a half-diminished chord. The second note of the Locrian mode is a weak tone. You can use the Locrian mode to improvise over the ii⌀7 in the minor II–V–I. Here is the G Locrian mode.

TRACK 150

You can think of E♭ Mixolydian instead of G Locrian because these two modes share the same notes, and G⌀7 and E♭7 are related chords. Use the E♭7 (dominant) bebop scale and related ideas over G⌀7. In more general terms, improvise over a half-diminished chord using the bebop scale (and related ideas) that begins a major 3rd below the root of the chord. Here is a line over G⌀7 using E♭7 bebop scale ideas.

TRACK 151

THE JAZZ MELODIC MINOR SCALE

The **jazz melodic minor scale** is often used to improvise over minor-major 7th and minor 6th chords. This scale is like a major scale but with a flatted third degree. It is played the same way up and down, unlike the classical version of the melodic minor scale that is played differently when descending. You can use the scale over the im(maj7) or im6 in the minor II–V–I. Here is the F jazz melodic minor scale.

TRACK 152

The jazz melodic minor scale has no weak tones. Here is an improvisation based on the F jazz melodic minor scale.

TRACK 153

Here are two good ways of leading to the tonic of the melodic minor scale.

TRACK 154

These are good ways to lead to the 3rd of the scale.

TRACK 155

If you combine these "leading" ideas with chord tones of a minor triad – in this case F, A♭, and C – you can come up with some great melodies. The following example shows an F melodic minor scale improvisation using "leading" ideas.

TRACK 156

Practice: Create lines from the jazz melodic minor scale using these "leading" ideas. Start with F minor and G minor to prepare for upcoming exercises and tunes. Once these are solid, begin learning the other keys.

In the following example, I have created lines over the minor II–V–I using the scale techniques covered in this chapter so far. The V7 chord in the minor II–V–I should be played as an altered dominant, so here's your chance to use the Jewish scale, as I showed you earlier. Later, I will show you other scales that you can use to improvise over an altered dominant chord.

TRACK 157

Practice: Learn to play these lines over the II–V–I in F minor as in the example above, then transpose to C minor and G minor before attempting to learn this material in the other keys.

Sometimes, a minor II–V is used to lead to Imaj7. The minor II–V prepares us for a minor chord, so the Imaj7 comes as a bit of a harmonic surprise. Here are some examples in the key of C. Notice that I am using B♭7 scale material on D°7. On G7, I am using the G7 Jewish scale, and on the Cmaj7, I am using the C major bebop scale and related vocabulary.

TRACK 158

77

THE ALTERED SCALE

There are a few more scales that are frequently used to convey an altered dominant sound. The **altered scale** is one of these. It goes by several different names, including the **diminished whole-tone scale** and the **super Locrian mode**. It is the seventh mode of the melodic minor scale. For example, the G7 altered scale uses the notes of A♭ melodic minor. In general terms, if you want to play the altered scale over a dominant chord, use a melodic minor scale that starts a half step above the root of the dominant chord.

Try playing the altered scale shown below. The scale contains three basic chord tones of a dominant 7th (root, 3rd, 7th) and all of the altered dominant extensions (♭9th, ♯9th, ♯11th, ♭13th). Dominant voicings used in conjunction with the altered scale can make use of one or more of the altered dominant extensions. These voicings should not include the unaltered 9th, 5th, or unaltered 13th.

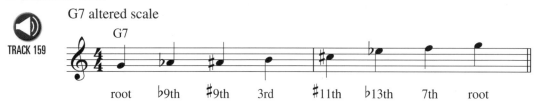

There is a classic phrase that comes from the altered scale that has become known as the "Cry Me a River" lick due to the fact that it is similar to the opening phrase of that tune. The altered scale most often leads to a chord that is up a 4th or down a 5th. The examples demonstrate that these altered licks can lead to chords of various qualities. Here are a few ways you can play this phrase.

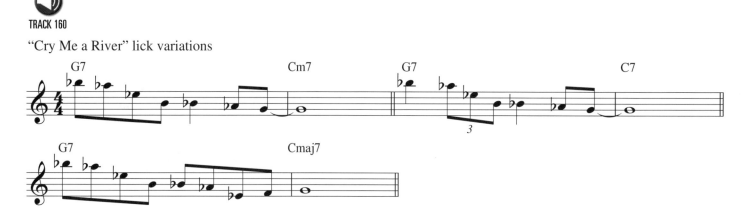

Practice: Learn the altered scale and "Cry Me a River" licks for G7, C7, and D7 before beginning to learn them in the other keys.

You can use four-note altered licks to lead to a chord that is up a 4th or down a 5th. Here are some examples.

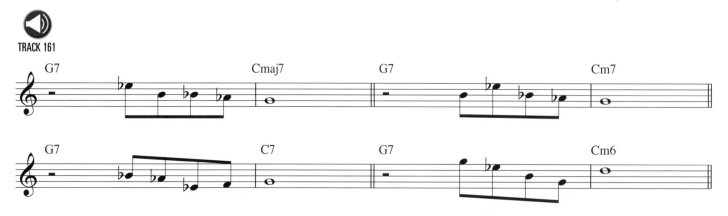

78

It is common to use a short altered phrase right before a resolution. Check out these examples, where I improvise with the dominant bebop scale over a iim7–V7 and then insert an altered lick for the two beats before the resolution to the Imaj7.

To create longer phrases with the altered scale, try joining four-note altered phrases together.

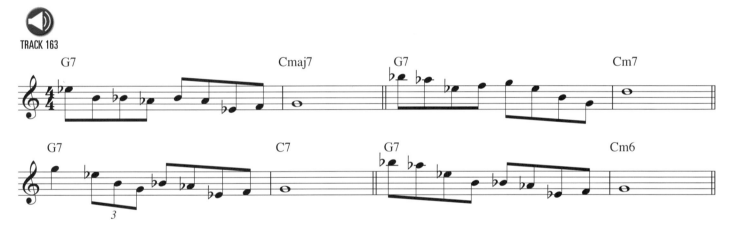

Practice: Create your own iim7–V7–Imaj7 lines that include these four-note altered licks. Form longer altered phrases by combining the four-note ideas.

THE DIMINISHED SCALE

The **diminished scale** can be used to improvise over diminished chords as well as dominant chords. It is an eight-note scale that combines the four chord tones of a diminished 7th chord with its four upper extensions (9th, 11th, ♭13th, maj7th), resulting in an alternating pattern of whole steps and half steps. Here is the C diminished scale.

Due to the symmetrical nature of the diminished 7th chord and the diminished scale, it is often said that there are only three diminished 7th chords and only three diminished scales. To understand this, play the inversions of C°7. You will get E♭°7, F♯°7, and A°7. All four of these chords share the same notes. Now try playing C♯°7 and its inversions. You will again come up with four diminished chords that share the same notes. Lastly, play D°7 and its inversions and you will again come up with four chords that share the same notes. Can you see that there are really only three diminished 7th chords? The same is true of the scales.

Here are three diminished scales. Any other diminished scale you play will share the same notes as one of these scales.

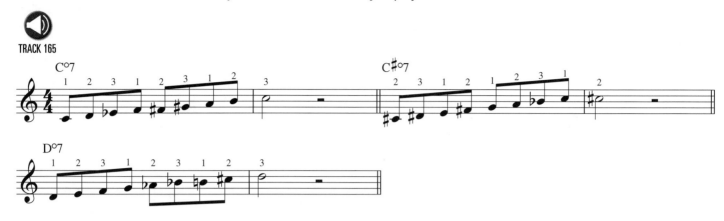

TRACK 165

When we ascend with the diminished scale, we typically begin on a chord tone, but when we descend, we typically begin on an upper extension. This allows us to retain the whole step–half step–whole step–half step pattern that "pulls" the line forward due to the **leading tones**. Play the following ascending and descending examples of the diminished scale.

TRACK 166

Practice: Learn to play the three diminished scales up from the four chord tones and down from the four upper extensions.

Let's take a look at how the diminished scale can be used with dominant chords. When a ♭9th is added to a dominant chord, its 3rd, 5th, 7th, and ♭9th form a diminished 7th chord and the root of the dominant chord can be viewed as an upper extension of that diminished 7th chord. For example, the 3rd, 5th, 7th, and ♭9th of G7♭9 are B, D, F, and A♭, respectively. These notes form B°7. The root of G7 is an upper extension (♭13th) of B°7. This means that G7♭9 and B°7 are related chords, so you can play the B diminished scale over G7♭9. The following example shows how the notes of the B diminished scale relate to G7♭9. Dominant voicings used in conjunction with the diminished scale can make use of one or more of the following extensions: ♭9th, ♯9th, ♯11th, 13th. These voicings should not include the unaltered 9th or ♭13th.

B diminished scale used over G7

TRACK 167

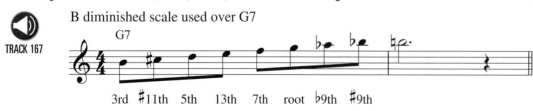

3rd   ♯11th   5th   13th   7th   root   ♭9th   ♯9th

The following lines are examples of how you can use diminished scales over dominant chords that lead to major, minor, or other dominant chords.

TRACK 168

Practice: Think of tunes you know that have spots where you could use lines from the example above. To gain mastery of vocabulary, it is important that you practice within the context of a tune. Simply practicing an idea in all keys won't necessarily mean you will be comfortable including it in your solos. Practice incorporating specific ideas and phrases into the tunes you are learning.

Because of its symmetrical nature, the diminished scale is a great source for patterns. The following examples come from the B diminished scale or any of its equivalent diminished scales (D diminished, F diminished, and A♭ diminished). These patterns also fit with the related dominants (G7, B♭7, D♭7, and E7). In the examples, I lead to Cmaj7, but you can use these patterns to lead to other chord qualities as well. Any phrase that comes from a diminished scale can be transposed up or down in minor 3rds to create a pattern. Study the following examples to understand this concept.

TRACK 169

Practice: What you can do with diminished patterns is endless, so pick one of your favorites and work on including it in appropriate spots in the tunes you are playing. Try other patterns and make up your own.

IMPROVISING WITH WHOLE TONE SCALES

Way back in Chapter 2, I told you about the two whole tone scales. The whole tone scale is yet another scale that can be used to improvise over dominant chords. It is less common than some of the other scales we have discussed, but Thelonious Monk used it extensively and made it a distinctive part of his style. Use the whole tone scale that starts on the root of a dominant chord. The following example shows how the notes of the G whole tone scale relate to a G7 chord. Dominant voicings used in conjunction with the whole tone scale can make use of one or more of the following extensions: 9th, ♯11th, ♭13th. These voicings should not include the ♭9th, ♯9th, 5th, or unaltered 13th.

TRACK 170

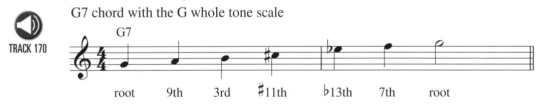

Here is an example of some of the linear patterns that can be created from the whole tone scale.

TRACK 171

Practice: Pick your favorite whole tone patterns and try to work them into tunes. Listen to recordings by Thelonious Monk to get ideas about where you might include them.

PUTTING IT ALL TOGETHER

The following is a solo on the chords of Cole Porter's "What Is This Thing Called Love?" I have incorporated all of the scales that were introduced in this chapter, as well as techniques from previous chapters.

TRACK 172

Chapter 10
MORE REPERTOIRE

VARIATIONS OF COMMON PROGRESSIONS

In Chapter 7, I discussed ways to improvise over Imaj7–vim7–iim7–V7 and iiim7–vim7–iim7–V7 progressions. Many jazz standards rely heavily on variations of these progressions that include VI7alt in place of vim7. The symbol "alt" suggests the use of the altered scale, however, I frequently use the Jewish scale as an alternative; either scale leads effectively to the minor chord that follows. It is optional whether you treat V7 as an altered dominant or simply leave it unaltered. Play the following line based on Imaj7–VI7alt–iim7–V7 and iiim7–VI7alt–iim7–V7 in F.

TRACK 173

Practice: Work on improvising over Imaj7–VI7alt–iim7–V7 and iiim7–VI7alt–iim7–V7 with one chord per bar as in the example above. Draw upon all of the different scales and techniques that have been introduced in this book.

Many tunes use Imaj7–VI7alt–iim7–V7 and iiim7–VI7alt–iim7–V7 with two chords per bar. Here is an improvisation based on these progressions in B♭. I have included a few new ideas.

TRACK 174

Practice: Work on improvising over Imaj7–VI7alt–iim7–V7 and iiim7–VI7alt–iim7–V7 with two chords per bar as in the example above.

JAZZ BLUES

Earlier, we discussed the three-chord blues. Unless this simpler form is agreed upon, jazz musicians typically use a more complex chord progression for the blues. Although there are countless variations, here is the typical jazz version of the blues. Notice that it includes Imaj7–VI7alt–iim7–V7. The last three chords are used to lead back to the top.

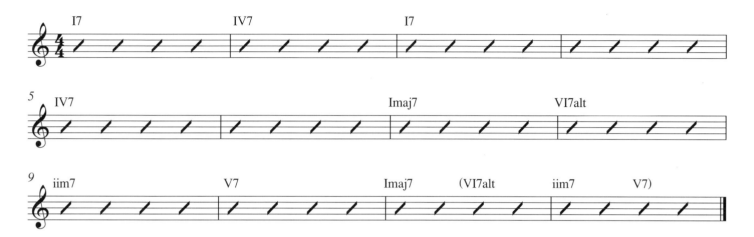

Here it is in the key of F.

TRACK 175

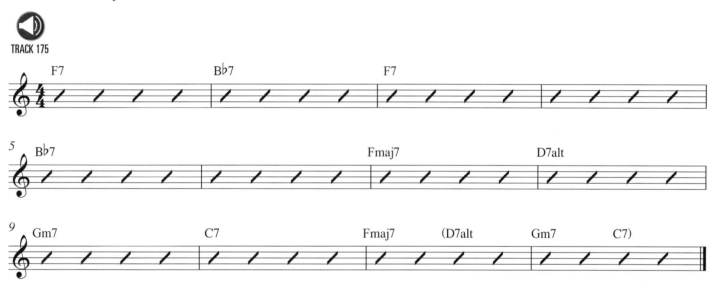

Here is an example of a solo on the blues using much of the material you have been learning. You will see some chords in parentheses. B°7 is the ♯iv°7 and B♭m7 is the ivm7. One or the other are sometimes included as a way of leading from IV7 back to Imaj7.

TRACK 176

The phrase I used in measure 6 is a nice way to move from B°7 to Fmaj7. This is a useful little idea that you will be able to use on other tunes as well.

TRACK 177

Practice: Improvise on the jazz version of the F blues. Learn an F blues head such as Charlie Parker's "Now's the Time" so you can play a complete performance. Work out ways of comping so you will be ready to play in a group. Learn the jazz version of the blues in other common keys such as B♭ and C.

RHYTHM CHANGES

Another important progression to get familiar with is **rhythm changes**. This is jazz jargon for the chord progression of George Gershwin's composition "I Got Rhythm." You can see why it is easier to just say, "Let's play rhythm changes!" Musicians often shorten it even more and refer to it as simply "rhythm." There are many tunes based on this progression and, as with the blues, there are endless variations.

Here is a basic way to play the progression. Notice that it includes Imaj7–VI7alt–iim7–V7 and iiim7–VI7alt–iim7–V7. The chords in parentheses are commonly used alternate chords. E♭maj7 (IVmaj7) is followed by either E♭m7 (ivm7) or E°7 (♯iv°7). Notice how these chord movements are similar to the chord substitutes I used in the blues solo earlier in this chapter (page 85, Track 176). The last three chords are used to lead back to the top.

TRACK 178

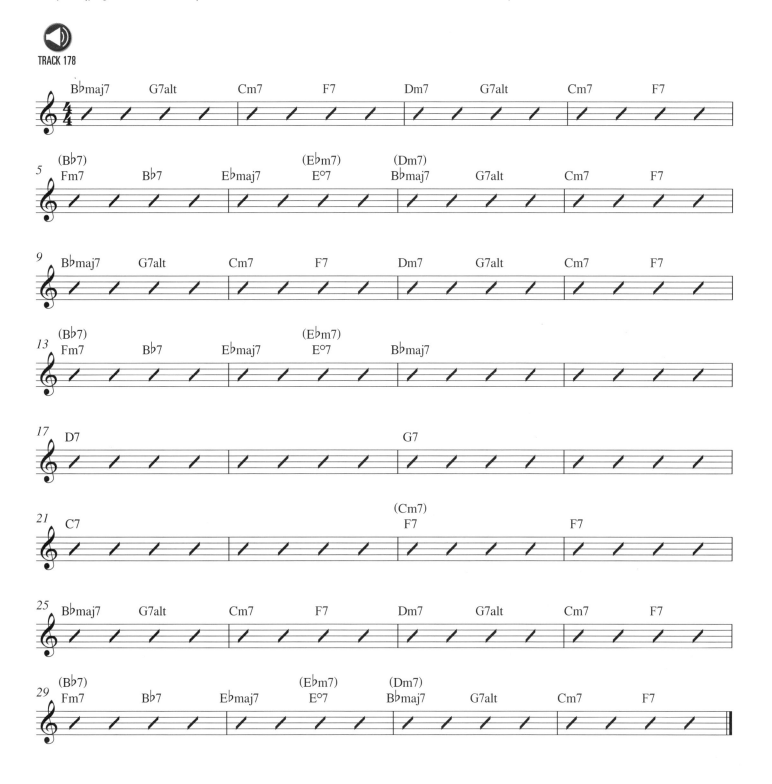

Here is an example of a rhythm changes solo that uses much of the material you have been learning. I structured this as an etude in order to demonstrate many ideas, so I didn't leave as much space as I typically would in a solo. In measures 6 and 14, I again use the diminished lick I showed you earlier (page 86, Track 177).

TRACK 179

Practice: Analyze this solo and use it to help you improvise your own solos. Start with very slow tempos, but gradually work up to faster tempos. Learn a rhythm changes head like "Oleo" or "Anthropology." Work out ways of comping as well. Be prepared – musicians like to play rhythm changes way up-tempo!

"Autumn Leaves"

Here is an example of a solo on "Autumn Leaves," a popular standard composed by Joseph Kosma. I made use of much of the material you have been learning. The E♭maj7 chord in measures 4, 12, and 24 functions as the IVmaj7 in the key of B♭. For this reason, I didn't change to the E♭ major scale in those measures; I simply continued using the B♭ major bebop scale and related ideas.

TRACK 180

Practice: Work on improvising on "Autumn Leaves." Learn the head and work out ways of comping. The blues and rhythm changes are two of the most commonly played progressions and "Autumn Leaves" is a frequently played standard. Once you become skilled at playing them, you will be able to transfer this knowledge to countless other tunes.

CONCLUSION

You're probably realizing, now more than ever, that the process of learning to play jazz piano is a never-ending journey. I hope this book has unlocked some of the mysteries of this music for you and that it has inspired you to continue to practice and listen. Sometimes it will feel like you are making rapid progress, but more often than not it will seem slow. Learning a new tune, discovering a new artist, hearing an incredible recording, taking in a live performance, and playing music with others will motivate you to continue your quest. Just keep at it every day and enjoy and appreciate the privilege of being able to play music. Over time, you will look back and be amazed at how far you have come and what you have achieved.

GLOSSARY

Aeolian mode: The sixth mode of a major scale, also known as the natural minor scale.

altered dominant tones (a.k.a. altered dominant extensions): The ♭9th, ♯9th, ♯11th, and ♭13th of a dominant 7th chord.

altered scale (a.k.a. diminished whole-tone scale or super Locrian mode): The seventh mode of a jazz melodic minor scale.

arpeggio: A broken chord, i.e., the notes of the chord are played in succession rather than simultaneously.

ballad: A slow tune.

bebop scales (a.k.a. jazz scales): Scales containing added passing tones, commonly used by Charlie Parker and others from the Bebop Era.

big band: A jazz group of 10 or more members.

blues (blues progression): A musical form, usually 12 measures in length, or any tune based on this progression.

blues scale: A minor pentatonic scale that often also includes the ♭5th.

bossa nova: A Latin style from Brazil.

bridge: The B section of an AABA form.

changes: Jazz musicians' term for the chord progression of a tune.

chart: A lead sheet or any written jazz arrangement.

chord: A combination of three or more pitches sounded simultaneously.

chord quality: Chord type (e.g., major 7th or minor 7th).

chorus: One time through the form of a tune.

chromatic scale: A 12-note scale of half steps.

comping: Chorded accompaniment for a melody or improvised solo.

cycle: A series of all 12 notes arranged in a pattern that moves up in 4ths or down in 5ths.

degree: A note within a scale, often labeled numerically to indicate its position relative to the tonic.

diatonic: Involving notes from a major scale (or related mode) with no chromatic alterations.

diminished scale: An eight-note scale that combines the four chord tones of a diminished 7th chord with its four upper extensions, resulting in an alternating pattern of whole steps and half steps.

diminished whole-tone scale: See altered scale.

Dorian mode: The second mode of a major scale.

enclosure: A melodic technique of leading to a chord tone or other target note by using notes that chromatically or diatonically surround it.

enharmonic equivalents: Two notes that are identical in pitch, but written differently (e.g., C♯ and D♭).

fake book: A book of lead sheets.

feel: Rhythmic style.

form: The structure of a jazz tune when played once through, not including an intro or special ending. Letters of the alphabet are often used to describe form and denote sections (e.g., AABA).

half step (a.k.a. semitone): The smallest distance between two notes on the piano.

harmonic minor scale: A type of minor scale that can be formed by flatting the third and sixth degrees of a major scale.

head: The melody of a tune.

idea: A short musical phrase that can be incorporated into a solo.

interval: The distance between two pitches.

intro: A musical introduction to a tune.

inversion: A chord arranged so that a chord tone other than the root is the lowest note.

Ionian mode: The first mode of (and identical to) a major scale.

jazz melodic minor scale: A type of minor scale that can be formed by flatting the third degree of a major scale. The same notes are used ascending and descending, unlike the classical version of the melodic minor scale that is played differently on the way down.

Jewish scale (a.k.a. Spanish scale): The fifth mode of a harmonic minor scale.

lay out: Stop playing.

lead sheet: A page of music that usually shows just the melody and the chord symbols of a tune.

leading tone: A note that resolves to a note a half step higher or lower.

lick: A short, often familiar, melodic phrase.

Locrian mode: The seventh mode of a major scale.

Lydian mode: The fourth mode of a major scale.

major scale: A series of seven notes that can be formed by ascending from any note using the formula: whole step – whole step – half step – whole step – whole step – whole step – half step.

minor pentatonic scale: A five-note scale, composed of the 1st, ♭3rd, 4th, 5th, and ♭7th degrees of a major scale.

Mixolydian mode: The fifth mode of a major scale.

modes: Scales formed by starting on each degree of a "parent" scale.

passing tone: A nonharmonic note that connects harmonic notes.

Phrygian mode: The third mode of a major scale.

progression (chord progression): A sequence of chords.

rhythm changes: Jazz term for the chord progression of George Gershwin's composition "I Got Rhythm."

rhythm section: The musicians in a jazz group that accompany and help keep time. The most common instruments in a rhythm section are piano, bass, and drums, but guitar and/or various percussion instruments may be included as well.

root position: A voicing in which the root is the lowest note.

rootless voicing: A chord, often played by the left hand, that does not contain the root.

scale: A group of notes arranged in ascending or descending order.

semitone: See half step.

seventh chord: A chord of four notes that can be stacked in 3rds.

shell voicing: A voicing that contains just the root, 3rd, and 7th (or 6th) of a chord.

slash chord: A chord played over a bass note other than the root. With this type of notation, the chord is indicated to the left of or above the slash, and the note required as the lowest is shown to the right of or below the slash.

smooth voice leading: Minimal note movement between voicings.

Spanish scale: See Jewish scale.

standard: A tune that most jazz musicians know. Many of them were composed for musicals or movies and some were composed by jazz musicians.

stride: A piano technique that involves the left hand playing a low note on beats 1 and 3 and a middle-register chord on beats 2 and 4 of each measure.

super Locrian mode: See altered scale.

swing (swing feel): A jazz style in which eighth notes are played with an alternating "long-short" rhythm.

syncopation: The rhythmic practice of placing notes or emphasis on offbeats.

tonic: The first note of the major scale, natural minor scale, harmonic minor scale, or melodic minor scale.

top: The beginning of the form of a tune.

trading fours or trading eights: Alternating brief solos of four or eight measures between two or more members of a jazz group. It is common for a horn player or pianist to "trade" with the drummer.

transcribing: Notating music you learn by ear.

transposition: The process of moving a note or group of notes to another key.

triad: A chord of three notes that can be stacked in 3rds.

tritone: An interval of three whole steps.

turnaround: A progression that leads back to the beginning of a section or to the top of a tune.

upper extensions: Notes that can be added to a four-note chord (e.g., 9th, 11th, and 13th).

vocabulary: Licks and phrases used in improvisation.

voicing: The particular arrangement of notes of a chord.

weak tone: A note in a scale that clashes with a related chord.

whole step: An interval of two half steps.

whole tone scale: A six-note scale of whole steps.

TRACK LISTING

Titles in bold are performed by a trio.
All other tracks are solo piano.

Mark Davis – piano
Jeff Hamann – bass
David Bayles – drums

Recorded by Ric Probst at Tanner-Monagle Studio, Milwaukee, WI.

Chapter 7: Major Vocabulary

Chapter 8: More Harmony

Chapter 9: More Scales

Chapter 10: More Repertoire

ACKNOWLEDGMENTS

Special thanks to my family, friends, and former teachers, for your support and guidance, and to my students, past and present, for inspiring me to continue learning. In particular, I would like to thank my good friend Rick Krause for his invaluable help with this book.

ABOUT THE AUTHOR

Mark Davis is an accomplished pianist and an influential educator who has been a mainstay on the Midwest jazz scene for over 25 years. He has performed with jazz luminaries Eric Alexander, Peter Bernstein, Slide Hampton, Jimmy Heath, Brian Lynch, Charles McPherson, Frank Morgan, and Phil Woods, among others.

Mark began classical piano studies at age eight and soon took to improvising and composing. His teachers at the Wisconsin Conservatory of Music included Adelaide Banaszynski and David Hazeltine. He later studied with jazz legend Barry Harris, who remains one of Mark's primary inspirations as a player and educator.

Since 1992, Mark has taught at the Wisconsin Conservatory of Music, where he serves as Chair of the Jazz Institute. He is also on the music faculty of Alverno College and Wisconsin Lutheran College. Many of Mark's former students have gone on to successful careers in music, most notably Dan Nimmer, pianist with Wynton Marsalis and the Jazz at Lincoln Center Orchestra.

Mark's previous work for Hal Leonard includes transcriptions for *Miles Davis: Kind of Blue* for their Transcribed Score series and numerous recordings for their *Real Book Play-Along* series.

For more information, visit www.markdavismusic.com.

TESTIMONIALS

I find Mark Davis's *Jazz Piano Method* to be informative and insightful, not only for pianists, but for all musicians. His wealth of knowledge about jazz piano is evident. His method and approach is interesting and well thought out. As one who does clinics and master classes, I'm always seeking new ways and methods to inform, excite, and motivate the students. I highly recommend Mark's book.

> –Dr. Charles McPherson, saxophonist (has worked with Charles Mingus,
> Barry Harris, Dizzy Gillespie, Jay McShann, and others)

What I like most about Mark's *Jazz Piano Method* is that it's a well thought through, logically organized, clearly articulated, and thorough approach to learning how to play jazz piano. Starting with the fundamentals of listening, standard forms, and basic scale and chord construction, Mark Davis clearly explains how to understand and practice the various aspects of jazz piano playing.

> –David Hazeltine, pianist (has worked with One for All, Jon Faddis,
> Slide Hampton, Louis Hayes, James Moody, Marlena Shaw, and others)

Mark Davis has put together a clear and comprehensive book that will give the student who goes through it carefully everything needed to enter and explore the world of jazz harmony. Mark is a great player as well as a great teacher who understands what fundamental knowledge and skills students need in order to create and to make their own harmonic discoveries.

> –Peter Bernstein, guitarist (has worked with Jimmy Cobb,
> Diana Krall, Brad Mehldau, Joshua Redman, Sonny Rollins, and others)

Mark Davis's book is a major achievement! Not only does it take the student through the basics of jazz piano technique, but it imparts the core concepts and skills of jazz improvisation brilliantly. Everything is well organized and presented in a no-nonsense, easy-to-follow sequence, and the exercises are well thought out. I would highly recommend this book not only to budding jazz pianists, but to players on all instruments who want to gain the functional piano skills essential to the complete jazz musician. I will be recommending this book to all of my students at the Frost School of Music! Kudos to Mark Davis – a gifted musician who can not only play it but also teach it.

> –Brian Lynch, Grammy® award-winning trumpeter (alumnus of Art Blakey and the Jazz
> Messengers, Horace Silver, Eddie Palmieri, Phil Woods, and others) Associate Professor
> of Studio Music and Jazz, The Frost School of Music at the University of Miami